Red Sky

A young girl's journey in Mao's China

Minzhi Xing

Copyright Minzhi Xing 2023

All rights reserved

Minzhi Xing

Printed by Ingram Spark

Print - ISBN 978-0-6457525-0-2

eBook - ISBN 978-0-6457525-1-9

This book is dedicated to my children who grew up in a completely different time and place.

Contents

Prologue	1
The Reunion	3
The Fields	10
Wenzhou	13
Father and Mother in the Cultural Revolution	24
Hong Qi (Red Flag) Primary School	34
Grandma	38
Gymnastics	48
Guangzhou is a Big City	67
No. 2 Middle School	76
Beginning University	86
Return to Wenzhou	92
South China University of Technology	100
Feng's Big Exam Time	110
Graduation	116
Gerhard	122
Gigi	137
Germany	147
Getting Married	154
Australia	165
Tiananmen Massacre	171
The Departure	179
Arriving in Australia	188
Epilogue	203
Acknowledgements	209

Prologue

I stood on the Pearl Bridge looking down at the dark brown Pearl River. The water seemed to be rushing somewhere, perhaps hurrying to join the South China Sea some 100 kilometres downstream. The neon lights on both sides of the banks were flashing vigorously. Even though in the 1970s there weren't many commercial advertisements on billboards on top of the buildings in China, Guangzhou was exceptional. Maybe because it was the largest city in southern China, and the closest major city bordering Hong Kong, Guangzhou was always a little more commercial than the rest of China.

It was a hot summer night; the winds were softly blowing my hair. Behind me, people were taking a leisurely stroll on the bridge, hoping to catch some of the coolness that was brought up from the water. Some were chatting, some just walking, some with bamboo fans, occasionally fanning themselves. Summers in Guangzhou were very hot; temperatures could reach up to 36 degrees with 98% humidity. In the middle part of the bridge, people on bikes were crossing the bridge to get home or wherever they wanted to go.

In the 1970s, Pearl Bridge was the only bridge linking the north and south parts of Guangzhou. It was 350 meters in length, 18 meters in width, and 182m above water level, consisting of pedestrian paths on both sides and vehicle and bicycle lanes in the middle. The Bridge, made of steel and concrete, looked very much like Sydney Harbour Bridge, with its metal half-moon-shaped frames on top.

I felt utterly alone among the crowds. All the people around me had nothing to do with me; they all had their own lives to live and homes to go to. Looking down on the water, I thought to myself:

'What would it be like to jump into the river now?'

'How deep is the water?'

'Would I be able to kick myself up to the surface? I'd probably hold my breath first, then I'd choke because I can't swim!'

'What does drowning feel like? Is it painful?'

'Can people who are able to swim still drown?'

'Probably not because people's survival instincts would kick in and they would float.'

'What would be the best way to die without pain?'

I had all these questions going through my head.

I was one month shy of turning 15, and I started to ask the question, 'What is the point of living?'

At that moment, a stranger came and stood next to me - he was a middle-aged man. He spoke something in Cantonese that I could not understand. I had only just arrived in Guangzhou a few months before and I did not understand a word of Cantonese. Cantonese is very different from Mandarin, which we learnt in school. Mandarin has four tones, and Cantonese has nine! People in Guangzhou all spoke Cantonese.

My thoughts were interrupted, and reality hit me; what did this strange man want? I was a bit scared, so I hurried home.

The Reunion

On March 16, 1976, Grandma, my younger brother Feng, and I arrived at the Guangzhou train station. After 8 hours by bus and 32 hours by train, we were all very tired. I have no recollection of the 40-hour journey - how we managed to get on the train, whether or not we had seats (because our station was not the beginning of the trip, and only people from the beginning of the trip had allocated seats), whether I had slept on the train, whether we bought food or what the food was like. How dirty and smelly was it on the train? No, I have no memory at all. I do not remember how we packed our bags and who saw us off at the bus station in Wenzhou where I was born and had spent 10 of my 14 years of life, without the presence of my parents.

People say, when you experience trauma, your body chooses to forget so you can get on with living your life. Whether or not the trauma surfaces sometime in your life down the track - that is a different story. This must be an occasion that my mind chose to forget. It was the second time in my short 14 years of life that I was forced to part with my family, friends, people close to me and my familiar surroundings, and was taken to a totally strange city; the first time was when I was five years old. I was living with my parents in Guangzhou then and as I was close to school age and my parents had no fixed home, they sent me to Wenzhou to live with Grandma. I don't remember the trip and how we got to Wenzhou then.

This second time, Mother must have met us at the train station, and Father was away on business at the time we arrived. I was 14 and a half years old, and Feng was 13. We had a very vague memory of what our mother and father looked like. We must have had their photos somewhere at Grandma's place, but I do not remember looking at them. All we knew was where they lived - a city called Guangzhou, nearly two thousand kilometres away from where we lived with Grandma in Wenzhou, the city mother was originally from.

Grandma, my brother Feng and I arrived in Guangzhou, reunited with our parents after 10 years of separation - 1976.

During those 10 years when we were with Grandma, I remember Father came to visit us once when I was about seven. Mother came twice; once was in 1967 when grandpa died, and another time was when I was 11, in 1972.

In China in the 1960s, children were commonly looked after by their grandparents because parents devoted all their time and energy to fulfilling the agenda of the Communist Party, such as the Anti-Rightist Campaign, the Great Leap Forward, and the Cultural Revolution.

Anti-Rightist Campaign, which lasted from 1957 to 1959, was a political campaign to expose alleged 'Rightists' within the Chinese Communist Party (CCP) and the country. The campaign was launched by CCP Chairman, Mao Zedong. First Mao encouraged people to voice their opinions and criticize what CCP did wrong and what should improve. Once these people did voice their opinions, they were punished and were named 'Rightists'. The Anti-Rightist campaign damaged democracy in China and turned the country into a basically one-party country.

The Great Leap Forward was an economic and social campaign led by Mao from 1958 to 1962. Mao launched the campaign to reconstruct the country from an agricultural society to a communist society through the formation of people's communes. Mao declared that grain yields yearly should be doubled and even tripled, without any scientific backups proving to be possible. Local officials were fearful of Anti-Rightist Campaigns and competed to fulfill or exceed quotas which were based on Mao's exaggerated claims, collecting non-existent 'surpluses' and leaving farmers to starve to death. Higher officials did not dare to report the economic disaster which was being caused by these policies and national officials, blaming bad weather for the decline in food output, took little or no action. Millions of people died in China during the Great Leap.

At the time, my parents were working in civil engineering. They were building roads and bridges all over the countryside in Guangzhou. They had no permanent home and stayed in tents in the fields. When a project finished, they moved on to the next place. All the belongings my parents had, I was told, were in two wooden boxes that my father had made.

Father and Mother were from two different provinces. They met while they were working in the fields. Mother studied civil engineering at Hangzhou Civil Engineering College in Hangzhou, the capital city of Zhejiang province (about 10 hours by bus from Wenzhou where Mother's family lived). There were about 90 who graduated from the same school. The entire group was sent by the government to Guangzhou to work.

Father was from a small village on Hainan Island in Guangdong province, China's largest island in the far south. He was a peasant. He worked on a salt farm on the island before he left home when he was 20 to study to become a communist leader at South University in Haikou, the main town of Hainan Island. Later he was sent to the same place as my mother to work.

Mother and Father met at work in 1956.

Father said that when he met my mother, Mother was very poor. *'Her washing basin had patches after patches of repairs; she couldn't afford to buy a new washing basin,'* he said. He felt so sorry for my mother *'that's how I ended up marrying her,'* he claimed.

They were married in Guangzhou in 1957. There was no wedding celebration, just a certificate from the registering office and a black and white photo.

A year later, Mother was pregnant with her first child. She gave birth to my elder brother, Miao, in Guangzhou. Grandma came to help mother and looked after Miao. She stayed for a year with mum and dad, leaving Grandpa alone in Wenzhou. However, the conditions in the fields where Mother and Father were posted, were too harsh to bring up the child. There was no running water, no toilet, no bathroom, and no kitchen; all they had was a tent. Therefore, Grandma took Miao back to Wenzhou. At least in Wenzhou, Grandma and Grandpa had a two-room house, rented from the government. Moreover, it was in the city, not in an open field in the middle of nowhere.

Two years later, my mother was pregnant with me. Again, she needed Grandma's help, so she went back to Wenzhou to give birth. On September 4, 1961, I was born at the Third Hospital of Wenzhou.

It was the year of the Ox. I was the only one out of us three children who was born in Wenzhou. Mother said the pregnancy with me was the most difficult one because she felt sick most of the time, while with my brothers she was not too sick.

Forty days after my birth, Mother returned with me to Guangzhou. At the time, women were given 40 days off work after giving birth. Grandma packed her bags and with my older brother Miao, came to Guangzhou to give Mum a hand with the two children. However, she could not stay long.

Worrying about Grandpa and her home, she left Guangzhou and took Miao back to Wenzhou again. I stayed with Mum and Dad in the fields.

*Miao and Me, before Grandma took Miao to Wenzhou
1962, I was 8 months old, Miao was 4.*

Eight months after I was born, Mum discovered she was pregnant again. She said it was an accident. They did not want any more children. She went to three hospitals trying to have the pregnancy terminated, however, the hospitals refused. At the time, China had not announced the One-Child Policy. In the 60s, Mao actually encouraged people to have more children because many people died during the Korean War, especially young men. That was why China's population doubled in just 20 years after 1949 when the Communist Party took over China. One of the scholars in China at the time, Ma Yinchu, a prominent Chinese economist and father of family planning in Chinese history, pointed out that it was a mistake on Mao's part to encourage people to have more children at the time. But his view was ignored, and later during the Cultural Revolution, he was punished for criticizing Chairman Mao.

(But in 1979, the Central Communist Party of China formally apologized to him. China's One Child Policy draws heavily on Ma's population theory).

So, my younger brother, Feng, was born in Guangzhou in 1963. Later on, when we returned to Guangzhou in 1976 and Feng was having a lot of trouble getting along with my parents; Mother said that maybe Feng knew that she had tried to get rid of him when he was still in her womb.

It was too much for my parents to cope with both work and children. So, they decided to give Feng to Grandma to look after as well. But they kept me with them, maybe because I was the only girl in the family. Out of three children, I was the one who stayed with Mum and Dad the longest.

Feng was only 11 months old when grandma took him to Wenzhou. Grandma said: *'he was the best baby, he slept day and night.'* He slept such a long time that the back of his head went flat. Later on, when we children fought with each other, we called him 'flat head'. He would get very angry with us.

My parents kept me with them until I was five years old. When the Cultural Revolution started in 1966, they sensed something big was going to happen, and it was about the time that I started school, too. So, they sent me to Grandma and my brothers, and I stayed in Wenzhou with Grandma for ten years - the ten years of the Cultural Revolution in Chinese history.

The Fields

I still remember some of the things that happened when I was little and living with my parents in the fields. I was about three when one night my parents were at a meeting and left me sleeping in the tent. A goat came near our tent and bleated. I woke up and found myself alone in bed in the dark. I screamed. Another night, I woke up at the wrong end of the bed. I could not find my pillow, so again, I cried. Mum and Dad were always busy with work and endless meetings.

3.5-year-old me on the bridge Mother's company built - 1965.

When I was about four, my parents sent me to a boarding kindergarten. I would go in on Monday mornings and come back home on Saturday evenings. I do not know where we were at the time. The boarding kindergarten must have been in a nearby town.

I had no recollection that I was put in the boarding kindergarten for the entire year when I was four until recently when I talked to Mother. I thought I was put in a daycare or something similar. Mother said that on Sunday evenings I would start to cry. Mother asked me why. I would say tomorrow I have to go to kindergarten again and I don't want to go. My parents would smile at me: *'You are a worrier,'* they would say. A four-year-old child started to worry about tomorrow.

Every Saturday afternoon I would stand at the gate waiting for my father to take me home. If he came late, I would ask him why he was so late while the other children were long gone. Father said I cried out *'Baba'* behind the gate with tears running down my face, and this would break his heart. In kindergarten, one thing I remember was the food. I couldn't eat the food there. Every time when other children had finished their meals, I would still have my bowl full of rice sitting in front of me untouched. The aunt (we called the carers in the kindergarten aunts) would come, shake her head, and take the rice away.

After lunch, we would be put to bed for a nap. There were at least 30 to 40 cots in the big room. I remember I always refused to sleep. I cried, but no one paid any attention to me.

Another time, I remember I jumped out of a window. The creche must have been on the hillside, I remember that the window was close to the ground. I wanted to go home, Mother later told me. I don't remember what happened afterwards. I must have been caught and returned to the room.

I did have some good times in the fields, though. *'You were pretty wild,'* Mother said. I loved running around in the open, playing in the creeks. I was very popular among my parents' colleagues. I always sang songs when they asked me to, and then they would give me some sweets.

Father took me to visit his parents in Hainan Island when I was about four. I was the only grandchild my grandparents met from my father's family. Father has three sisters and one brother. He is the eldest and he was the only person in his family who left the village and lived in the big city. Because he is the eldest, and he was earning a wage, he felt responsible to support his family in the village. From when I could remember, Father always sent part of his wages to his parents every month after he received his pay. Father did not talk about his family much and us kids never asked.

I vaguely remembered the trip to Father's hometown. They lived in a very old mud and hay house. It was very dark and dreary. Father said the first night I slept in the bed I was bitten by insects and fleas, so he had to hold me in his arms to sleep for the rest of the nights we were there. But I remembered the sweet potatoes. I just could not get enough of them.

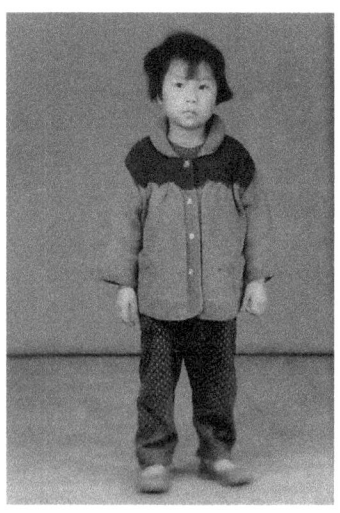

1965 before Father took me to visit his hometown, Hainan Island. I was four.

Wenzhou

This map shows the position of Wenzhou, Guangzhou, Hangzhou, Dalian (where my aunt lived) and Hainan Island where my father's family was from.

My parents decided to send me to Grandma in 1967, to join my brothers Miao and Feng. I was five years old.

Wenzhou is located in the southeast corner of Zhejiang province, surrounded by mountains and the East China Sea. Because of the location (76% of its surface area is classified as mountains and hills), back then in the 1970s, it was very difficult to travel anywhere from Wenzhou by land. The only transportation to go to the nearby city would be by bus, going through cliffs and tunnels in the mountains. There was also a ship that would take 24 hours on the East China Sea to get to Shanghai. We called the ship the Big Ship; it was a great deal if you heard about anyone who took the ship to Shanghai back then.

My mother and her three children, taken when she brought me to Grandma in Wenzhou - 1967.

Grandma's house occupied two rooms downstairs in a timber complex of a double-story building - no bathroom, no kitchen, just two rooms. Symmetrically opposite us, there was another family that had similar two rooms. The two families shared an undercover common space. We later partitioned this space into two parts and built our brick stoves on each side of the partition, which became our kitchen. We had our tables next to our stoves and that would be our dining area. There was a courtyard in front of the complex, in which there was a well where we collected our water. Our complex ran off a blue-stoned lane called Seven Star Halls Lane.

There were six of us in the two-room house. Together with me were Grandpa, Grandma, my two brothers and my cousin Ching. Ching is the oldest daughter of my mother's younger sister, Aunt Meijun. She was living in another city called Dalian, in the northern part of China - another 1500 kilometres away from Wenzhou. Grandma had two daughters. My mother is the older one, Aunt Meijun is four years younger than Mother. Mother left home at 17 to study bridge design at Hangzhou Civil Engineering College in the capital city of Zhejiang

Province. Aunt Meijun went to Beijing to study to become a teacher. She was later sent to Dalian in northern China after she finished her studies and has lived there ever since. So, in the 1950s, my grandparents were left by themselves in Wenzhou. This was quite unusual in China because, in China, we took pride in big families. Children live with their parents and look after them when they grow old. But my grandma was different. She encouraged her daughters to go to school and to have a good career. She did not complain at all when they left her and Grandpa behind. She told them not to worry about her and Grandpa. Even when they had their children, Grandma would take up the responsibility to look after the grandchildren. She wanted our parents *free from worries, just concentrate on work.*'

A few years later, we were joined by another cousin - Ching's little brother, Hang. He was the one I felt very attached to later because I was the one who looked after him. I was the eldest girl among five children. Grandma was so busy with all the housework that she let me take care of Hang's daily life. I dressed him in the mornings and washed him before he went to bed. I bathed him, played with him, taught him songs (he had a beautiful voice when he was little, and he learned to sing quickly), and I wiped his bottom. We shared the same bed with grandma. He slept at my feet at the other end of the bed. Once I accidentally scalded his hands, and another time when I wanted to visit my best friend, I tried to lose him when he followed me. I smacked him when he didn't listen to me, as well. I was nine and he was two.

Grandma never worked, as far as I remember. Grandpa worked at a boiler factory. He died of a fatal stroke at the age of 55 in 1968, when I was about seven.

I do not remember much of my grandfather. The only thing I

remember was before he had the stroke, five of us children had some photos taken in a photo shop. They were good photos (mine was the one with me proudly holding Chairman Mao's little red book). Grandpa was happy to see those photos. He had some drinks the night he had a stroke and died two days later in hospital.

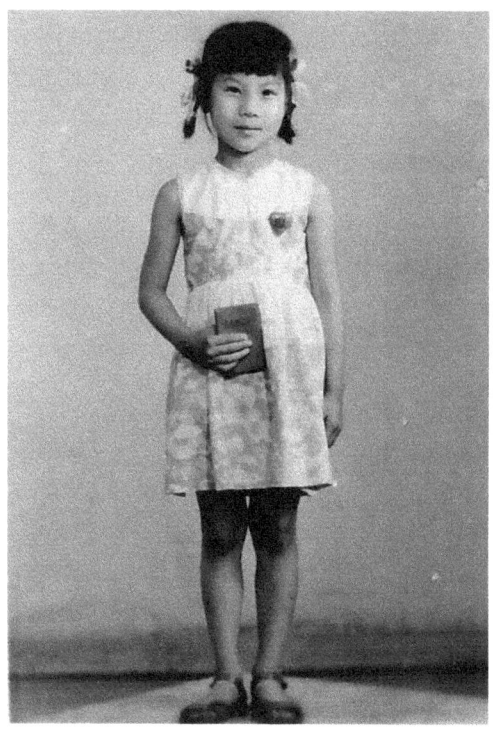

6-year-old me holding the Red Little Book and wearing a heart-shaped badge that says 'loyal' which means loyal to Chairman Mao - 1967.

I remember the funeral. He was placed in the coffin, and we put the coffin in the middle of a room. Relatives would come and kneel in front of the coffin, burning paper money so that he would have money to spend in his world and he could look after us who were still in this world. Later, the coffin was put on a tricycle, and we all walked slowly through the streets behind the coffin. Then we came to a river where we all got into boats, took the coffin, and were taken downriver into the countryside where Grandma's family was buried. Grandpa's parents were originally from Fujian province - the province opposite Taiwan. They didn't have his grave ready for him in Wenzhou. Grandma was originally born in Wenzhou. Her ancestors had bought a hill in the country as their graveyard. Grandpa passed away so suddenly that he had to be taken to Grandma's family graveyard to be buried.

Grandpa's grave was what we called a 'bun grave' because it looked like a steamed pork bun. People with money would have their graves built like an armchair. We called those 'armchair graves'. Mother and Aunt Meijun came for Grandpa's funeral. They cried in front of his grave.

Grandma, Grandpa (front, the only photo I can find of Grandpa), Aunt Meijun and one of Grandma's brothers.

Grandma did not seem to miss Grandpa much. She later told me that their marriage was arranged by matchmakers. Grandpa's family used to have money. They had a mine producing Alum to serve the local people. One thing I remember about Alum was that we used it to clear the water from the well. If the water from the well was dirty, we used it to stir the water round and round on the surface and after a while, the dirt would sink to the bottom, and we would be able to use the clear water. In those days, not many people in Wenzhou had running water. Water was generally not treated, so Alum was commonly used to purify it. Therefore, Grandpa never needed to work until the communists took over China. Then, while escaping from Wenzhou to Fujian province where his parents had settled after the Japanese invaded China, the ship that his family was on was robbed by pirates who stole all their possessions including gold nuggets, Grandma's jewellery, clothing, and furniture. *'Everything was gone,'* Grandma said. She wanted to jump into the sea, she said, but Mum and Aunt Meijun grabbed her from behind and would not let go of her.

One night, not long after Grandpa died, I woke up and found Grandma crying desperately. That was the only time I remember her crying.

We were left with no income, Grandma and five children aged from one to ten. My parents and Aunt Meijun sent us money every month. I remember my parents would send 60 Chinese Yuan each month. At the time, one Yuan would buy about two kilos of rice, which would last us for two days. Half a kilo of soy sauce cost 20 Jiao, which was 0.2 yuan. Aunt Meijun would send 15 Yuan. If we had not had to buy those ration dockets, things would have been much easier.

When the Communist Party took over in 1949, China was a very poor country. There was simply not enough food to feed the whole country. So, the CCP introduced the Ration system. People were given ration dockets to buy limited rice, meat, oil, sugar, coal, cotton, etc. The Ration system lasted for more than 20 years and was lifted in 1984.

All daily provisions in China at the time were strictly rationed. This meant everybody who was legally registered to live in that city would have a fixed amount of daily supplies - such as the essentials listed above. Between the six of us, Grandma and my elder brother Miao were the only ones who were registered in Wenzhou. The rest of us were what we called *'black citizens'*, which meant we were not supposed to live in Wenzhou. It was illegal for us to live in Wenzhou, and we would have been sent away if the officials had found out. Our registration was with our parents in Guangzhou and our cousins with their parents in Dalian.

Being *'black citizens'* caused us many sleepless nights. There were times when officers from the city's security bureau came to the household during the middle of the night to check for people who were not registered with the city. I do not know how we survived those checks. Every time we would be very scared. Grandma was nervous, too.

Consequently, six of us lived on rations for two people. Life was a constant struggle. Everything was in short supply - rice, coal, sugar, meat, fabric, and money, of course. We had to use the money to buy those dockets from the black market.

Grandma often asked relatives or neighbours to lend her some money and she would always say: *'When their mother sends some money, I will return it to you immediately.'* I felt ashamed every time I heard Grandma begging people for money.

Water was also a problem. There was no running water in the household in Wenzhou at those times. There was usually one tap with what we called 'automatic water', in other words, running water, at the end of a lane or street. We had to use a tin bucket to buy water. Carrying buckets of water, from my memory, was the most painful job that I had to do.

We had two tin buckets; each held about 25 litres of water. When I turned seven, I started to carry one bucket with my elder brother. We had a bamboo stick, and we would tie the bucket in the middle of the stick, each putting the ends on our shoulders, one in front, one at the back, carrying the water home. Every household had a big terracotta water container. Every two or three days we had to fill the water container, which held five or six buckets. And that was only the cooking and drinking water. For washing clothes, we had to get water from a nearby well. Or when we had heavy rain, we would put all our tins and buckets under the eaves to catch the rain for later use. I was always happy when the rain came.

Aluminium water tins for carrying/buying water.

I always complained when I had to carry water. Miao used to yell at me. He was the eldest male in the family. Even though he was only 10, he carried all the responsibilities of the household on himself. One time in winter, it was bitterly cold and windy (winter in Wenzhou could reach below zero degrees), and I had to go and fetch the water again. After walking in the wind, I developed a rash all over my body. It was what we called a wind rash, or what we call it nowadays, cold-induced urticaria. My whole body swelled up and I ended up in the hospital.

For hot water, every household would have at least two or three hot water bottles to store hot water for tea or washing. Because there wasn't enough coal, sometimes we had to save the coal for cooking our main meals, so we would go to a special hot water shop to buy hot water.

Apart from the hot water, the shops sometimes sold lollies and puffed rice. I do not know whether they were run by the government or by private families. Probably the government had some arrangements with the families who ran them.

The stoves to boil hot water were built specially and were big. On top of the stoves, there were huge woks with round panelled timber tops. On one side of the timber, there would be taps. You would put your bottle under the tap and serve yourself. It usually cost one fen, about one cent, per bottle.

One evening, also in winter, Grandma asked Miao and me to go and get some hot water. I was about nine years old. I was carrying only one bottle by the handle. It was very cold; I didn't have gloves and my hands went numb. On the way back, we had almost reached the front yard of our house when I wanted to change hands, the handle slipped away from my numb fingers, and I dropped the bottle on the ground. The hot water did not burn me, but the sound of the explosion of the glass thermal bottle shocked me. I was in tears when I told Grandma that the hot water bottle was broken.

Grandma was angry with me. Not only did we not have enough hot water that night, but we lost a hot water bottle, which was quite costly, as well. She picked me up, put me to bed, and smacked me on my bottom. That was the only time

I remember Grandma smacking me. I was upset, and I felt I was misunderstood. But I couldn't say anything.

Hot water bottles (thermal) (Left)
Wooden containers sitting on top of a big Wok selling hot water (Right)

Apart from the physical difficulties in life, spiritually and emotionally we were quite happy in Wenzhou.

When the snow came in winter, I remember I would sit behind the window watching the white flakes slowly fall down from the sky and land on the roof of the opposite house. Day by day, the snow would accumulate to about 20cm high on the roof and the ground. Then we would go out and make a snowman or throw snowballs at each other.

In summer when we had heavy rains, the streets would be flooded with water. This was great fun. We loved walking in the yellow water with our pants rolled up to our knees. Sometimes we would bring out our wooden basin that was used for baths and sit in it, letting the water carry us away.

No families had bathrooms in Wenzhou at that time. Every family would have one or two big wooden basins for a bath. There was a city bath that opened every winter where you could buy a ticket and have your bath or shower. It was considered a luxury treat. But my family never used it. Grandma said it was dirty. Later on, when I joined the city gymnastic team, we were given free tickets to go and have showers or baths there. I enjoyed the advantage that I was given.

For a toilet, each family would have a wooden container that had a lid. Almost all of them were round in shape. Some were bigger than others. Families used this container as a toilet. There was a special wooden box, also with a lid, in which you could put the toilet or leave it out. You could also sit on the edge of the box. Every two or three days, very early in the morning, there would be a person with a two-wheeled barrel and a big wooden tank on top of the barrel who came to collect the waste. He would pick up the containers one by one and pour the waste into the tank. We considered the waste collection job to be the lowest job one could have. Later, during the Cultural Revolution, many intellectuals were forced to do this job. Then Grandma would wash the container and chat with the neighbours at the same time. Later on, I did that job and I hated it.

Wooden chamber for toilet

Father and Mother in the Cultural Revolution

In 1966 the Cultural Revolution started in China. Its movement affected every corner of every city. A small town like Wenzhou was no exception.

The Cultural Revolution was a socio-political movement in China from 1966 until Mao Zedong's death in 1976. It was launched by Mao, the Chairman of the Communist Party (CCP) and founder of the new China (People's Republic of China). Its stated goal was to preserve Chinese communism by purging remnants of capitalist and traditional elements from Chinese society. Mao called on young people to 'bombard the headquarters' and proclaimed that 'to rebel is justified'. The youth responded by forming Red Guards and 'rebel groups' around the country. A selection of Mao's sayings were compiled in the Little Red Book, which became a weapon to denounce those so-called 'anti-revolutionists'. The revolutionary committees often split into rival groups and became involved in armed fights and violent 'class struggles'. The Cultural Revolution was characterized by violence and chaos. Death toll claims vary widely, with an estimate of those perishing being from 250,000 to several million people.

Miao was at primary school in 1967. A week after the term had just started, the school had to close because a gun battle broke out between two groups of political ideologies. Our home was like a bomb shelter. We pasted our windows with strips of paper just like the English flag. The reason for doing this was so that people would not be hurt by broken glass in case a bullet shot through the windows. I remember this because the shape of the paper strips was exactly like the Chinese character for 'rice米(mi)'. Every morning when I woke up, the first thing I saw was this big '米' on the windows. What would a life be like if only we had plenty of rice every day? After that, even now, whenever I see the English flag, that window with paper strips appears in my head. We even hung our quilts over the windows to stop the bullets from coming through. Stories about people who were shot in the streets or at home, whether deliberately or by accident, were heard everywhere. One story went like this: while a person was lying in bed, a bullet came down through the roof and shot him between the legs. He was lucky to be alive.

The actual shootings did not last long, maybe less than one year. But the Cultural Revolution lasted 10 years! During those 10 years, while we children were growing up with Grandma in Wenzhou, with the struggles of daily life, our parents were suffering physically and emotionally in Guangzhou. They were isolated, physically beaten, emotionally humiliated by their colleagues, and forced to do heavy labour because they supported the workers who criticized some of the bureaucratic leaders. It was common during the revolution for people whose views differed from the bureaucracy to be regarded as political enemies.

The construction company that my parents worked for was divided into two political groups. Those who had power usually sat in their offices drinking tea, writing letters of praise or condemnation of subordinates, or playing cards. They called themselves 'The Eastern Wind' which was the good wind as it opposed the things coming from the West. The other group consisted of those who mostly worked in the fields - like workers, foremen, technicians, etc. They called themselves 'The Red Flag'. Red represents the Communist

Party. For anything related to Chairman Mao or the Party, or describing loyalty to the Party, people would use 'hong', Red, in the names. You would find many Chinese people born during the 1960s have 'hong', Red, in their names. People even refer to the places where the Communist Party took place or had meetings as Red Villages, and the sky under which Mao led the Party to victory as Red Sky.

My parents belonged to 'The Red Flag'. They said they did not even know how they became involved. They always sympathised with the working class, they said. You could not stand in the middle; you had to take sides. Everybody was involved in one group or the other. In the beginning, everybody approved of the Cultural Revolution and thought it was a good thing. Chairman Mao asked the people to voice their opinions (again) of the Party and its leaders. '百花齐放，百家争鸣'; 'Let A Hundred Flowers Bloom, Let A Hundred Schools of Thought Contend'; to feel free to criticize.

'East Wind' and 'Red Flag' felt free to advertise their differing views in posters, which they pasted on walls, notice boards, and wherever they could find the space. The posters were what we called 'Big Posters'. People went out every night to read them. At first, the posters were personal political views, but later, as the Cultural Revolution progressed and the disagreement between the two sides grew, they started to criticize individuals. The situation deteriorated even further, and the arguments became fiercer. People started to exaggerate in order to destroy their opposition. Anyone could write a big poster about anyone or anything. There was no law to protect people's private lives. They even wrote about who slept with whom and when; whether it was true didn't matter. Anything that would destroy the other side's reputation would be invented. I even remember that in one of the busy streets in Wenzhou, one of our neighbours wrote a big poster about our grandma. I cannot recall the content now, but I remember we never spoke with that family again after that. Grandma even moved house for that reason. I never understood why people would write anything about Grandma. She was just a very busy housewife who was trying to bring up five hungry children. She was never involved in any political issues.

By 1968, the Cultural Revolution was out of control. It was not just a poster war. The two parties started to fight physically, using fists, bamboo sticks, iron rods and guns. The East Wind people had the power and the weapons. The Red Flag group, made up mostly of workers and farmers, was defenceless. Some people from the Red Flag party tried to break into the security bureau to steal guns to protect themselves. They were arrested and beaten. Their colleagues tried to rescue them, and that created more conflict. There was no right and wrong in those days. The whole situation was out of any group's or anyone's control. People were lost in a huge movement that was like a big wheel rolling down a hill faster and faster that couldn't stop.

Everywhere people were being arrested and beaten. Father realised that this was not how it should be. He didn't like violence. Fighting was wrong. But there was nothing he could do to stop it. People were mad. So, he thought of retreating to Hainan Island where the village was remote and probably quieter. He bought a ticket for the ship. He was going to go to the village to stay there for a while. No one paid any attention to work in those days. Mother was called back to Wenzhou at the time because of Grandpa's funeral. We children were safe with Grandma. So, Father decided to avoid the violence. He wrote a letter to Mother asking her to stay there as long as possible; not to come back until he notified her.

But it was too late.

On July 23, 1968, on the ship on the way to Hainan Island, Father was arrested. Not by police, but by his colleagues, people who belonged to the 'East Wind'. He was dragged off the ship that a few minutes later would have delivered him to safety. He was taken back to the base where immediately he was forced onto his knees. Twice someone hit him on his back with a heavy stick.

He was denounced as an 'anti-revolutionist', 'the son of the landlord', 'capitalism's running dog', etc. They hung a big timber sign on his neck with five names written on it. They used a very thin chicken wire to hang it around his neck. He was expelled from the communist party, the party that he thought would serve its people well, in which he had firmly believed and for which he had worked so hard.

They shaved his hair into a cross and then painted it with red paint. Father tried to convince them that he was none of the names that they gave to him, especially the one, the son of a landlord. He tried explaining that for many generations his family had been peasants, very poor peasants. They never owned a single piece of land. If they had checked the records of his files, they would have realised that it was wrong to accuse him of being a son of a landlord. For this, he received a kick in the stomach. Who cared what was true and what was not at that time? The whole country was going insane.

Father was jailed in the 'Cowshed', which meant he was under arrest in a separate room. He could do nothing without permission. He managed to ask a colleague to send a telegram to Mother. He dared not tell her the truth because he knew the telegram would not reach her if he did. In the telegram, he said 'Niece Qing is seriously ill and is in hospital; won't be able to get out until she is better.' He intended to let Mother know that he was in trouble, implying that she should not come back. But the telegram did not reach her. It fell into the hands of his persecutors. Later it was used as another excuse against him. He was accused of trying to stop Mother from coming back to participate in the revolution, to receive 'thoughts reform'.

Meanwhile, Wenzhou was also in chaos. The transport system had broken down. Mother could not go anywhere anyway. The company she worked for did not care. They wrote her letters one after another asking her to return. Her pay was stopped. A final order came, ordering her to return by a set date and threatening that they would 'take an action' if she failed to comply. Mother knew clearly, what the 'action' meant. There was no way she was going to avoid the confrontation. Delay might cause harm to the family. She was certain that they would come to Wenzhou to get her if she resisted. After two months in Wenzhou, she bought a ticket to return to Guangzhou.

As soon as she stepped from the boat that took her to the town in which the construction headquarters were situated, she saw, across the bridge on the other side of the bank, her colleagues kneeling in a line being denounced. She knew things were not going to be easy. But this scene was still a shock to her. She walked back to her tent and put down her luggage. As she walked through the streets, some of her co-workers saw her and looked away, avoiding her gaze. A few men came after her and immediately she was taken to an office. They shaved her hair into a cross. Then she was taken out to the streets and forced to denounce herself whilst loudly banging a tin bowl with a spoon. One man poured a tin of red paint over her head.

The names my mother was called were similar to Father's, except she had two more - one was that she was called 'a snake in the grass', and the other was 'class enemy'. All this meant she was an enemy of the communists. These names were all derived from an incident during Mother's days in high school.

When Mother was about 14, she was in middle school. She participated in a Russian literature study group, which she thought was simply a study group. Later it turned out that this study group, according to the Communist Party, was connected to a party that was anti-Communist, but Mother did not know this at the time. She naively thought she was actively involved in 'revolution' - whatever revolution meant to her.

After the communists took over China, she experienced all sorts of obstacles in her study and work because of this 'black spot' in her history. Firstly, she was refused entry into the college that she applied for in Wenzhou, although her score was one of the highest. Instead, she went to a less prestigious college, which later merged with Hangzhou Civil Engineering College. She was one of the top students in her college, but no one dared to make friends with her at school because they feared the consequence of associating with her. In her second year at the college, she was taken by the security authority to undergo political rehabilitation classes. Her own studies were stopped for a year. After graduation when she was working, the pay was classified according to qualifications and results and she should have been paid top rates, but she was not. The reason was that she was considered to have once been 'anti-Communist'. Mother held her tongue through all those years, *'Like a dog putting its tail in between its legs,'* she said.

Again, during the Cultural Revolution, this history was brought up.

When Father saw Mother kneeling there with her hair shaved

and hands tied behind her back while he was walking out towards the stage being denounced again one day, his heart broke. He was in despair. *'This is it,'* he thought to himself, *'this will be the end for both of us. One is not enough, they want two.'*

There were about 20 of them who were arrested. Every day after lunch and dinner, they would be taken to this so-called 'denunciation meeting' and put on their knees, wearing the heavy signs in front of them, their heads lowered to their chests. People would yell at them, spit on them, hit them, and kick them; anything they felt like doing. Sometimes they were all tied together and dragged along the streets. Other times they were put into a truck that had an open platform. The truck was driven slowly through the streets to let everyone in town see that these were the people who wanted to 'overthrow' the communists. They wanted to stir the people up into hating them. Anybody was permitted to bash and humiliate them. *'Those animals knew where to kick.'* Father said. *'They deliberately aimed at your liver, stomach and kidneys.'* They were kicked from one side of the room to the other like balls. The screaming and yelling could be heard from afar. A number of times, Father thought he was going to die.

In those days, nobody knew how many people were tortured to death. Near the construction field, there was a river called the Western River. Every day there were corpses floating down from the upper stream. Some had no heads, some no legs. Father told me that many students were bashed to death, too. They were the sons and daughters of the 'anti-revolutionists'. During the Cultural Revolution, according to different estimations, one to seven million people died across China. Most were tortured to death; others were suicides. But the real number could never be known.

Apart from the torture, during the day they still had to work.

They were forced to do the heaviest labouring work on the site, such as carrying rocks, soil, and heavy machinery. Concrete bags weighing 25 kilograms each had to be carried two at a time. Mother said she did everything, from climbing 30 meters high to tie the bamboo as a support platform, to jumping into a hole that was 15 meters deep to mix the concrete as well as using heavy machinery. Even much heavier, stronger workmen admired her ability. She was equal to any men. She was only tiny, less than 150 cm tall, weighing 45 kg.

Father said they were so used to being tortured that they even joked about it. Every day after meals, one of his colleagues would yell out *'time to dress up!'* That meant putting on their heaviest clothes and as many as they could. They hoped that the thick clothing would reduce the impact of a punch or kick. They were forced to write so-called 'self-criticism', too, which meant that they had to write what they had done and why it was wrong. Father said it was so humiliating to have to invent the things that you had never done and then to slap your own face to say that you did it and it was wrong. You had to invent something or be punished, Father said. *'Close your eyes, grit your teeth, just write and write.'*

Father had malaria at one stage; his temperature went up to 40°C. No one even bothered to take him to the hospital. He was left to die. In the end, some of his colleagues who used to work under him quietly carried him to the hospital and saved his life. He was sick for 30 days.

They were tortured twice a day every day for 180 days. Father said.

The skin on my father's knees went rotten because of the kneeling. Later on, when he had an X-ray, it was discovered that one of his ribs was broken. He suffered physical pain even after the torture stopped. He has had trouble breathing ever since. They were lucky to be alive, Father would say.

The physical scars faded slowly, but emotionally, both my mother and father have never recovered from their experiences. The pain, the humiliation, the insult, and the anger inside has affected their lives forever.

And their pain extended to us later when we returned to live with them.

At the time that this was all happening, we children knew nothing about it. We were happy in Wenzhou with Grandma, although life was a struggle at times. My parents were grateful that we stayed with Grandma in those years, otherwise, there would have been no one to look after us. As the children of so-called anti-revolutionaries and 'class enemies', we too would have been denounced and abused.

Hong Qi (Red Flag) Primary School

Father came to visit us in Wenzhou when things quietened down a little. The year was 1970. I don't remember much about my father's visit. All I remember was that he was very quiet; we didn't talk much at all. One night, Feng and I had a fight because both of us wanted to sleep with Father. Feng punched me in the stomach, which really hurt me badly, and I don't remember who ended up sleeping with Father in the end.

Father only stayed for five days, and then he went on to Hainan to visit his parents, our grandpa and grandma. I forgot all about him and Mother again. Life went on in Wenzhou. I was in grade three then. I had always been an average student in my class at primary school. If the top score was 100, I would always get between 65 to 80. The teacher said that if I could concentrate more, my score would be a lot better. She told Grandma that I always seemed absent-minded; kind of lost all the time. I was quiet and shy.

One day in grade two, in the middle of a lesson, a teacher came in with an attractive girl dressed in a white shirt and a yellow hand-knitted vest. The teacher said her name was Wei and she was transferred from another school. It turned out that Wei lived just minutes from where we lived. Later we always walked to school together. We were put in the same after-school study group, and we have been best friends ever since.

There were four or five people in our after-school study group, according to where we lived. We usually went to Wei's house because her family had the biggest house among our group. They had three big rooms, plus a kitchen, and lived upstairs. Most of all, they had running water in their kitchen. I was so envious of her living conditions.

Wei and I in 1973. We were in grade five.

Sometimes we went to another member, Hong's place, to study because there was no adult in her home.

Hong used to live with her father, mother and one little sister at the back of a government post office. The place where they lived was originally a storeroom which was situated in the middle of the building - therefore, there was no window. I remember we were all terrified every time we walked into her home because we walked into the dark. Even though it was a bright sunny day outside, her big room would still be totally in darkness. Hong would always walk in front of us to switch on the light - the only light hanging down from the ceiling in the middle of the room. Even when the light was on, because the room was big and the light was dim, we still couldn't see the walls of the room, so we were still scared.

Hong's father was denounced as anti-revolutionist during the Cultural Revolution. He was not allowed to work. He was jailed in a 'Cowshed' in the countryside and his pay was stopped automatically. We never saw him. Hong's mother was sent to the countryside to have her 'thoughts reformed'. She was allowed back once a month. She took Hong's little sister with her because she was still very young. Hong was always alone, but she looked after herself well. She was extremely capable, and she ate everything.

One time, at our school, we were having a 'don't forget the past' day. We were provided with a bun, which was made of what we called 'wild grass' (edible grass or herbs). We were told that when the Communist Army was having their Long March during the fight with the National Party in the 1930s, the wild grass buns were the only food they had. The 'good life' we were having now all came from the hard work of the Communists. We should not forget the past, so that was why we were given those bitter buns to eat.

I had one bite, couldn't swallow it, and threw it away quietly while there was nobody around. But I saw Hong not only had her share but also grabbed any buns from other kids who did not want them. I wondered how many days she hadn't had anything to eat.

We had some good times in those study groups. When we finished our homework, we would play together or just talk. Our group got along very well. I didn't want to go home, as I liked being with friends. Grandma did not mind if I came home a little late in the afternoon.

Our primary school was originally called Guangchang Street Primary School. During the Cultural Revolution, it was renamed Red Flag Primary School. There were 56 students in my class. All our desks were arranged neatly - seven rows and four columns. Each table was shared by two pupils, one boy, and one girl. Short people sat at the front, tall at the back. We had subjects like Chinese, Math, Music, Drawing, Politics, and Physical Education. Different teachers taught different subjects. The teacher who taught us Chinese was our classroom teacher. She taught us from grade one to grade four. Then we had a different teacher, but we didn't like the change; we were so used to our first teacher. Actually, later on when we had our class reunions, we would always invite our first teacher.

I was not at the top academically at primary school, but outside, in the schoolyard, I was always popular. I was good at playing with the ropes, the rubber bands, chase and catch, and all sorts of games we used to play. Those were the things that got me noticed by the other students.

Grandma didn't ask us about our school much. She was too busy with the housework. When she had a little bit of time between meals, she would always read a novel for a while.

Grandma

I could not find any photos of Grandma while we were in Wenzhou. This photo was taken in Guangzhou when Grandma took us to be united with our parents - 1976.

Grandma was everything to me. She was the log I hung onto in the endless sea, the supporting pillar of the house. I was terrified whenever she was sick or feeling pain somewhere in her body. The night when I saw her crying in bed beside me when Grandpa died, I was terrified. When she woke up with a toothache (which happened very often), I was scared. Sometimes her feet swelled up so she couldn't walk, and I would panic. What would we do without Grandma?

Grandma

One day in the early morning, Grandma had gone to the market to do the daily shopping. I was having fried rice that she had cooked for our breakfast before school. A stranger walked into our complex (there were 4 families living in the complex) and asked if there was an old lady who lived there. He described what she looked like. I knew it was my grandma. All of a sudden, I had this panicked feeling all over me again. *'No'*, I thought, *'No!'* He said she stepped on a rope in the Market, fell and had broken her arm. *'Where is she?'* I asked.

He said he didn't know. Someone had helped her up. He happened to be passing by in the market and asked Grandma where she lived and thought that he had better come and tell the family.

I did not know what to do. My whole body went cold. It was like the end of the world to me. I stood there trying to think. I was about 12 at the time. Then I remembered a few relatives whom Grandma and I often visited. I ran all the way to an aunt's house; she was a teacher at my primary school. She wasn't there - only her grandma was there. She was totally deaf and didn't understand what I was saying. I yelled and waved my arms but still couldn't get my message across. She just looked at me, puzzled, probably wondering what on earth was this young girl so upset about.

Then I thought of a friend of Grandma's who lived just next to the market. I ran to her home. The moment I got upstairs, I saw Grandma sitting there beside a table, with one arm in a sling hanging in front of her. She was having some noodles that the friend had cooked for her.

She looked up at me, and said lightly as if nothing had happened, *'What are you doing here? Why aren't you in school?'*

I couldn't speak. *'At least she is still alive!'* I thought. I felt such a relief.

I often had bad dreams, dreams about Grandma being dead. The nightmares just would not go away. I guess I was worrying all the time.

One day, Grandma was cooking and I stood by the stove, watching her stir-frying some vegetables.

I asked, *'Grandma, dreams are the opposite, aren't they?'*

'What do you mean?' she said.

I took a deep breath: *'I mean, when you dream a person died, that person will live longer, won't she?'*

She smiled: *'I don't know. Who did you dream was dead? Was it me?'*

Tears ran down my face as I walked away.

Not like other children's grandmas, my grandma was educated. She went to school for three years. She read novels whenever she had a spare moment. She read them even when she was on the toilet. I do not know where she got those books from, but she always seemed to get them. She loved novels that had happy endings, especially sad, tragic love stories that turned out fine.

Every morning before she went to the market and we kids were still in bed, she would come to our bedside and ask each one of us what we would like to eat that day. I always said meat, Feng would say bean curd, and Miao would say vegetables. Although we didn't have much money and there was never enough food, every meal was prepared carefully. Grandma was a very good cook. We always had at least 3 or 4 dishes every meal. The quantity was little, we were only allowed to have limited amounts, like two small cubes of meat, two vegetable balls, etc. but every dish was delicious. We had a variety of food too, even seafood like fish and crabs, occasionally.

There were five kids in our extended family. Grandma was the only adult. One can imagine how much work there was. I never saw her panic or get impatient. She looked after us the best she knew how. There wasn't much communication between her and us like western families do. She never asked us about our schools, friends, or anything. The cultures were different. Perhaps she was just too busy.

I always felt lonely and always liked to be with friends. The after-school study group gave me some of the company that I needed. I also spent a lot of time with Wei's family. Wei's father worked for a company in charge of sugar and cigarettes. He knew my family always had difficulties making ends meet. He would sometimes give me some quota dockets for sugar. I was very grateful to her and her family.

My friendship with Wei was very simple. We didn't do many things together. We were very different. She was not at all good at sports. But academically, her scores were always good. She was calm and well-organized. I was always absent-minded, leaving things here and there. When we were together, she was the one who always talked. I just listened. When she organised things like get-togethers, I was always the participant. I was like her shadow. Later on, when she dropped out of middle school because her mother didn't want her to be sent to the remote countryside when she graduated from high school (all high school graduates had to go to the countryside to help the farmers in the villages in those years; this went on for ten years during the Cultural Revolution), I became the stronger one.

I was good both academically and athletically when I reached middle school. Then she admired me and respected me a lot. Our friendship remains to this day.

Wei and I went to the photo studio to have this taken in memory of our friendship just before I depart Wenzhou for Guangzhou. In the photo, the words said 'farewell'. - 1976

Our parents would write to Grandma, but Grandma never told us anything, nor read their letters to us. She probably thought we were too young to understand anything. We had no idea what they were doing at the time. We just knew that they were living in a city called Guangzhou. I never questioned why our parents didn't want us to live with them. My older brother sometimes wrote to them because he was the eldest and he could read and write then. Actually, he was the only one who wrote to our parents regularly. I remember I wrote to them once when I became a teenager and realised that I didn't have any decent clothes. I asked my parents to buy me a floral shirt and a sports top. They wrote me back saying I was too young for a floral shirt. But they bought me a sports top. I was a bit disappointed, but a sports top was good.

Miao took on the role of the man in the family. We all had to listen to him. He would do the housework by himself first, and then he would ask us to do it. He watched our behaviour as well.

Once, we were having a meal and I didn't like certain foods (I was always fussy about food when I was young). He asked me to eat it. I refused. He threw his chopsticks at me. We all used aluminium chopsticks at the time. The chopsticks hit my head. I had a big lump on my head, but I still refused to eat the food. I was the one, they said, who was the most stubborn. After all, my zodiac was the ox, which is well known for its stubbornness.

But I admired Miao. He was always the number one in every area at school. At every assembly at school, he was the one who always sat on the stage with a red scarf around his neck (the *'Little Red Guard'* that the Communists created; in middle school, it was the *'Red Guards'*. You wore a red band on your arms). He was also selected for the school dancing team and was always the lead dancer.

One time, Miao's school went to the countryside to *'learn from the peasants'*. They were walking on a narrow country dirt road. A tractor came towards them. The tractor swung sharply when the driver saw a group of students walking on one side. It turned so quickly that the hook on its tailgate grabbed a teacher's backpack. She was dragged many meters. All the students panicked. Miao saw it and ran to the back of the truck and pulled her off the hook. Her nose was cut and hanging there, he said. And there were many other injuries as well. She died later in the hospital. Grandma and Miao went to the school for her funeral. She was very good to Miao, we all knew, and so young.

Since I was the oldest girl, looking after cousin Hang was my responsibility. Ching is Hang's sister. She is only one year younger than I am. But she didn't stay with us for long. Aunt Meijun took her back when she was nine.

My two brothers, Miao and Feng, with Cousin Ching 1966, before I arrived in Wenzhou.

I must admit that Hang was an easy boy to look after. He was quiet and obedient most of the time. He was about two or three, I was nine or ten. In the morning when he woke up, he'd yell out, *'I'm getting up!'* Sometimes I came to him immediately; sometimes when I was in a bad mood, I would deliberately delay coming to him. He would continue yelling until I came to dress him.

Don't get me wrong, we got along very well. I liked him. I washed his face twice a day and washed his feet every night before he went to bed. Feeding him was Grandma's job. He was a fussy eater, too.

One evening when Grandma was out visiting some relatives, the electricity went out (it happened very often). I was in a bad mood. I had to wash him again. I took the kettle off the stove and put my hand on the kettle. It didn't seem to be hot. Therefore, when Hang put his hands in the basin as I poured the water, I didn't stop him. I was a bit concerned, but I didn't think it was that hot. The water in the kettle was hotter than I thought. He started screaming immediately. I was terrified and didn't know what to do. A neighbour rushed over and put soap on his hands. Poor Hang, his hands were all red. He didn't have to go to hospital, but it was painful enough for him to cry for a long time. I felt guilty. I still feel guilty even today when I think of him.

My best friend Wei had a younger brother. He was one year older than Hang. Sometimes when I went to Wei's place, I would take Hang with me so he could play with Wei's brother. Hang was the youngest in our big family. He was five years younger than my brother Feng. We didn't play with him very often, so he was always alone. He didn't go out into the street and play with neighbours' children much because we didn't want him to. *'There are bad boys in the streets,'* we would say. He stayed inside most of the time.

One day I wanted to go to Wei's place. He wanted to come with me, but I didn't want him to. He followed me. I was aware of that so I walked as fast as I could to lose him but then I was worried when I got to Wei's place. I thought he might have gotten lost in the streets. I didn't stay long and hurried back. He was home and upset. He didn't want to speak to me until I cheered him up. Another time when he didn't eat his dinner properly, Grandma locked him in the room, and I let him out.

In 1971 when I was in grade four, one day, a teacher announced that a few gymnastic coaches from the city sports committee were coming to our school to select future gymnasts. She said anyone who thinks he or she is good at tumbling or splits should go to the school hall to be tested.

A few kids stood up and walked out. I wanted to go because I knew I could do the splits, cartwheels, and handstands without any problems, but I was too shy and not confident enough to volunteer. Fortunately, a student who knew me pointed at me and told the teacher that I should go. The teacher asked her if she was sure and then ordered me to go to the hall.

I learned those skills from Miao who was a dancer in his school dancing team (he later became a choreographer). We practised splits, bridges, cartwheels and so on, and did our handstands against the timber wall of our house under the window.

In the school hall, there were about one hundred kids from grade four to grade six, and we were asked to do the things I mentioned above. In the end, a few kids were chosen to form together with children from other schools, the first gymnastic team in Wenzhou. I was one of them and I was the youngest.

Gymnastics became a very important part of my life and played a very important role in my growth.

In 1972 Mother came to visit us. This was when the Cultural Revolution had quietened down; Mother came back from the Cowshed. I don't remember much of her visit. I only remember the departure.

Grandma

1972 - Mother came to Wenzhou to visit us. She looked sad, after all the torture and humiliation she endured during the Cultural Revolution. She could hardly smile, even in a photo shoot.

Mother was going to take the bus to Jinhua where she would take a train to get to Guangzhou. Grandma and I walked her to the bus station. I wanted to go with her. I got onto the bus and didn't want to come down. I was 11. When the time came, I had to get off the bus. I was angry. I was sad. I felt helpless and walked away with my hands covering my eyes. I cried. It was a rare occasion where I remember that I cried.

Gymnastics

The Wenzhou gymnastic team consisted of a girls' team and a boys' team for ages between 10 and 13. There were two coaches for the girls' team and one for the boys. We trained in the same hall and were the pioneers in gymnastic history in Wenzhou. The team was formed in 1971. Our girls' team coaches were Coach Xia and Coach Hu.

At first, we trained twice a week after school on Thursday and Saturday afternoons. During the first couple of months, there was test after test. The aim was to reduce the numbers and select the best people to stay on in the teams.

One afternoon before the meeting that would announce the list of who would go and who would stay, two friends and I went to a park to have some gymnastic photos taken. We did this before we had to return the uniforms that we were given to us as members of the city gymnastic team in case we were not chosen (I always thought that I would be kicked out).

When we got back from the park, we were late. The meeting had already started. In the end, two out of the three were selected to stay; one had to go. I was lucky enough to stay.

That was the last selection. Later, Coach Xia told me that the two coaches had different opinions about my staying in the team. Coach Hu said I was too young, too small, and too absent-minded. But Coach Xia saw potential in me. She said I was very clever and quick in learning new skills. I wondered why I liked Coach Xia better.

We trained every afternoon after school following that selection.

In 1972, the first provincial non-professional gymnastics competition took place in Wenzhou. Non-professional means we were not paid by the government to be trained as gymnasts. I still remember the competition, which was held at the city basketball stadium with thousands of people watching. I was so nervous that I fell off the beam (a lot of us did!). At the time, the competition rules were different; we were allowed to have a second try if we thought our first attempt was not performed well on the Beam. Coach Xia asked me to put my hand up to have a second try on the beam. I refused because I was so scared of so many people watching. She asked me again. When I refused again (I was always stubborn) she was disappointed.

The result came days later: I came 8th out of the hundreds in the province in my age group. The first seven were qualified to participate in the National Gymnastics Competition that would be held in Shanghai the following month. I just missed out.

I felt disappointed and upset with myself. I should have listened to my coach! At the time, I was very fond of my coach Xia. She liked me, too and was the one who insisted that I stay with the team.

During the competition week, all gymnasts stayed in a hotel. This was so we would concentrate more on training and focus on the competition. One thing I remembered very well, was not quite related to the competition. At the hotel, when we had meals, all the gymnasts and coaches from one team (boys and girls were separated) would eat together. For the whole week, I had been going to the canteen with Coach Xia and I always sat beside her. On the last evening, when it was dinnertime, Coach Xia didn't turn up at the hotel (she had a home and a son to go to). I waited and waited, but she still didn't come.

She stayed at home instead of the hotel that night. I didn't have my dinner that night and I was upset. I felt Coach Xia betrayed me, but I didn't tell her. How could I tell her that I did not have my dinner because she did not come back to the hotel? It sounds ridiculous!

I was 11 years old at the time. Thinking back now, I felt sad. Someone I liked wasn't there all the time for me. She wasn't my mother. What could I have expected? If my mother was with me, would she be there for me all the time? I don't know. I don't have the answer because I had never had that experience.

No one was there for me. Grandma was there and she loved us selflessly, but she was so busy. She showed her love by doing all the things for us like cooking, shopping, washing, etc. That's what I learned, too. You do things as much as you can for people when you love them.

During the following month when the coaches took the girls and boys to Shanghai for the national competition, we 'leftovers' had a great time in Wenzhou. Boys and girls 'trained' (actually, played) together; we didn't know what danger was. We tried new skills that were supposed to be supported by the coaches, but we supported each other. It didn't matter whether or not we knew how. We were wild and had so much energy to burn off.

Once, I did a backward somersault in the air. The boys were supposed to support me when I landed, but they missed me. I landed on my back and my head hit the mat so hard that I thought I broke my head! But I got up all right.

The second provincial gymnastic competition took place in Hangzhou, the capital city of Zhejiang province, in the summer of 1973. It was my first time being in Hangzhou. I loved the city. Hangzhou is famous for its charming, man-made West Lake which I loved, and our hotel was right across from the West Lake. In the morning when we got up, looking out of the window, there was this mist that covered the lake. It was so enchanting. I felt that I was in a dream.

There were many things to buy in Hangzhou, too. Like small bamboo baskets, paper fans, and things you wouldn't see in Wenzhou. I bought some gifts for my friends in Wenzhou. I bought Wei a beautiful paper fan that could be folded and put in a pocket. It had beautiful a Chinese painting on it.

I came 5th on both the floor and vaulting. Our team came first, ahead of more than 10 teams. I took home three beautiful notebooks with floral plastic covers (two for apparatus, one for the team) as my prizes. That year when Cousin Ching came to visit us from Dalian with Aunt Meijun, she was envious of my notebooks and insisted that I give her one. So, reluctantly I did. I have kept those notebooks to this day (plus the ones I earned the following year, I had seven notebooks altogether). They reminded me of the time when I was happy, accepted, and acknowledged for my hard work.

Apart from the provincial competition, which was held once a year, there were a couple of performances that we had to do in Wenzhou, which would normally be held in the city basketball stadium (where the first provincial competition was held). We would do our routines on different apparatus, one at a time, with thousands in the audience watching (not like the competitions when gymnasts perform on all apparatus). This was to show the people in Wenzhou what our gymnastics team was like. I loved all other apparatus except the beam. I fell off the beam almost every time. To finish the night, there was usually a tumbling show on the floor, to see who could do the most backflips. One time I remember I did 14 back handsprings in a row. Everyone in the audience clapped their hands and I walked back feeling dizzy, but proud.

With each performance, we gymnasts would be given a voucher that allowed us to buy breakfast from a couple of shops. We could select from sweet or savoury steamed buns and all sorts of fried dim sums made from flour. They were very delicious. I was always happy when we had those performances. Without those dockets, my family could simply not afford to buy any dim sums from the shop. Those dockets were such a treat for me.

One night when I came back from one of these performances, as I approached the lane where our house was, I saw a familiar figure standing under the streetlight. The wind blew up her clothes like a balloon.

'Grandma! What are you doing here at this time of the night?' I called out.

'I thought you'd be scared walking alone into our lane in the dark. So, I came here to wait for you,' she said.

'Oh...' I was so moved that I was speechless. Tears started to well up in my eyes. I managed to swallow them. Grandma didn't see them of course. I was about 12 or 13.

The third competition also took place in Hangzhou. This time I came fifth all around, third on floor and vault, and first on bars (bars were my favourite apparatus). The year was 1974, and I graduated from primary school.

One afternoon, a few weeks after we came back from Hangzhou, during the afternoon training session, a person from the city sports committee came to our gym and informed us that I was to represent the provincial team and participate in the national Competition in Suzhou, which is about an hour away by train from Shanghai (three hours from Hangzhou). I was the only one from our girls' team that was chosen. A boy from our team qualified as well. The boys' coach from our team was going to accompany us to Hangzhou. We had to be in Hangzhou within two days to join other gymnasts from all the other cities, train for three more weeks, and then head for Suzhou for the competition. The first seven gymnasts of two different age groups of girls and boys from the provincial competition would represent Zhejiang province to participate in the national competition, altogether 28 gymnasts and two coaches. The coaches were all from the State Institute of Gymnastics.

For some reason, the boy and the coach from our team weren't going to travel with me. I was a little scared at the thought that I had to travel on my own without an adult's company. I was 13. I had to take an eight-hour bus ride to Jinhua, then walk to the train station from the bus station (which was not too far, by then I had already been to Jinhua twice, so I knew how to get to the train station from the bus station), buy the train ticket, get on the train, get off the train at Hangzhou, and try to get to the institute where I was going to stay.

But, in the end, it turned out that there was a basketball team who were going to Hangzhou for a competition, so I went with them, and all my worries disappeared.

We arrived at Hangzhou safely. I don't remember how I got to the institute; all I remember was walking into the institute by myself with my luggage on my shoulder after the bus dropped me off somewhere. I didn't know where I should report to. I saw a staircase and started to walk up the stairs. A girl stopped me. I recognized that she was a gymnast from the older group. She recognized me as well, so she took me to the 4th floor, which was the top floor where our younger girls' room was.

All seven girls stayed in one room with four double bunks. I was the last to arrive, all the other bunks were already occupied, and my bed was next to the door. I chose the lower one; no one was on top of me. There were a couple of running shoes on my bed when I arrived, so the girl who took me there asked the other gymnasts to take their shoes off. She was about 15; older than we were. She was in charge of showing new gymnasts to their rooms, so she had a bit of authority. I put my bags down and sat on my bed (no mattress, just bare timber). The other gymnasts arrived earlier and already knew each other quite well. They just nodded their heads when I walked in and kept talking in a dialect that I couldn't understand. I felt quite lost at that time.

I remembered that one girl from Wenzhou who was admitted to this state sports institute to become a professional gymnast earlier that year also lived in this building. I found out which room she was in and went downstairs to look for her. She was there; this put my heart at ease a bit.

It was dinnertime. I was tired and hungry after travelling all day, but no one told me anything about dinner, where we should get our meals, or where we were going to train, etc. Official training hadn't started yet.

I remembered there was what we called an 'ice shop' just down the road. The ice shop only opened in summer to sell cold things like icy poles, ice cream, cold red bean, or green bean soups. It was late July, right in the middle of the hottest month in Hangzhou, so I decided to go to the ice shop to get something to eat.

Grandma gave me 10 yuan (about two Australian dollars) for the trip. She said she would send more money to me later. So, I had 10 yuan in my pocket. I had never handled that amount of money before in my life. All I had spent before was, at most 10 or 20 Jiao to buy some lollies and popcorn in the street shops.

I bought a bowl of iced red bean soup, which cost 40 Jiao. That was my dinner for that night. That evening, I felt sick. I touched my head. I knew I had a temperature. I told my school friend (she was one year younger than me). She did not know what to do either, but she said I had better tell my coach the next day. I slept with her in her upper bunk that night. The single bed was too small with the two of us in it. Neither of us slept well. I don't know why I didn't want to go to my own room upstairs. I had this feeling that my roommates didn't like me.

We started training the second morning. I still had this temperature, so I told our coach, Jiao. She put her hand on my forehead and said, *'only a little bit of temperature. Don't worry, today we are having a test; when we finish the test, you can go to the clinic to see a doctor.'*

I got through the test with a struggle (and I ripped the skin on my hands when we were on bars, too). I came sixth in that test, *'worse than the competition last month'*, I thought.

By the time I went to the clinic in the afternoon (the institute was a self-contained place with its own canteen, school, clinic, etc.) my temperature was very high. The nurse put a thermometer into my mouth and said, when she took it out,

'*39.3 degrees*'. She gave me a penicillin injection and told me to come back for another one in the evening.

The clinic was about a 20-minute walk from where we stayed. After dinner, it was already dark, and I hadn't asked anyone to come to the clinic with me, because I didn't know anyone except the friend from my hometown. She was not in the team that was going to represent Zhejiang Province to participate in the National competition next month. So, I went to the clinic by myself. It was only the second day after I arrived in Hangzhou. All day travelling yesterday and a test training today and I had a temperature. I didn't feel well at all.

Getting to the clinic was okay; it was the injection and the trip back that I'd never forget in my life.

Halfway through the injection, somehow the nurse could not push the liquid any further. The pain was such that I felt I was going to faint. The nurse had to take the half-emptied needle out; she didn't know what had happened. I sat there for at least 20 minutes before I could move my right leg. I dragged my leg all the way to my dormitory. The street seemed endlessly long. Thinking back, perhaps the nurse pricked the needle on my bone. I was very skinny then. For many years, after that injection, when I sat down, sometimes I could still feel a sharp pain on the spot where the needle went in.

Coach Jiao was a very beautiful lady. She had long hair plaited at the back. Her skin was white and smooth. She was only 22 at the time. I liked her the moment I met her. She had a boyfriend who was in the army basketball team at the time. Sometimes he came to visit her when we were training. He was tall and very handsome. We called him Uncle Chen.

I became very fond of Coach Jiao. I worked very hard. Not

because I wanted to win, as I didn't think of the competition that much, only because I wanted to please Coach Jiao. She liked me too; she said that I had always been more mature than the other gymnasts and that I had 'brains'. She didn't have to give many instructions to me. I'd do it properly. She never yelled at me; she just shook her head sometimes when I didn't do a skill well, and smiled. I worked harder. I did not want to let her down.

At the beginning of the training in Hangzhou, I was in the fifth position (I think that was the reason why those gymnasts in my room looked down upon me) in my group of seven gymnasts. By the end of the month, after three weeks of training, I came first. The other gymnasts still didn't like me because I worked hard, and Coach Jiao always praised me. They were, most likely, jealous.

The training was really intense, especially in the hot summer. The temperature was 36 to 40 degrees Celsius during the day, 33 degrees at night and humid, too. It was not too bad at training during the day, but at night, it was impossible to sleep. Our room was on the top floor and the concrete roof and walls radiated the heat that was absorbed during the day. I tossed and turned and just could not sleep. My back swelled up with a serious heat rash. A couple of times I got up, walking past Coach Jiao's room to get some water. She had her door open and saw me. Later when we handed our diaries in for her to look at (every gymnast had been given a notebook. We were asked to write diaries every day for coaches to read so the coaches would know what we were thinking.), she would write things such as 'sleep well' or 'have a good rest'. I lost a lot of weight during that month, which was good for a gymnast.

The only thing I didn't like during this month's training was the early morning training sessions. The bell would go off at 5 o'clock in the morning. Everyone would get out of their beds, put on their shoes, and run out immediately.

On the first morning, I didn't know what was expected. I brushed my teeth and washed my face first. I didn't feel comfortable meeting people without having my teeth brushed and face washed in the morning. I did them hurriedly, of course. By the time I got downstairs, Coach Jiao was looking at her watch with seven girls lined up in front of her. She said quietly, 'We have waited for you for ten minutes.'

I didn't brush my teeth or wash my face anymore after that when we had to have our early morning training sessions. After training, everyone would be sweaty and dirty anyway. No one would notice I hadn't brushed my teeth or washed my face in any case.

Another thing I hated was long-distance running. It was part of our strength training. I was always last, no matter how hard I tried. I could never win in distance running. I was good at short runs. I would sprint with all my energy (good for vault), but when it came to long-distance running, I was defeated. Coach Jiao would, in the end, shake her head and sigh with a smile.

Because I didn't know how to handle money and I thought Grandma would send me more money later, I spent all my 10 Yuan in the first 10 days. I don't remember what I spent it on. The only thing I remembered was that I bought a lot of sugar - pure white sugar. In Wenzhou, we only had two supplies for the six of us in our family; all of us kids liked sweet things. We used to put sugar on top of rice and eat the rice just like that. For the whole month's sugar supply, we would finish our quota in two days, so sugar was always in short supply in our family. At the State Institute of Gymnastics, we had this privilege that there was no limitation to the amount of sugar we could buy. So, I bought a lot!

Grandma didn't send any money. Instead, a neighbour happened to be visiting Hangzhou and she asked her to bring me a small box of snacks. It happened during an afternoon training session. Coach Jiao said to me that there was someone outside who wanted to see me. I went out and recognized the neighbour who gave me this small box. I didn't know what was inside at the time. As it was in the middle of training, I didn't open it. In the evening when I did, it was full of my favourite snacks. I especially remembered the green bean moon cakes. They were so beautiful and tasted delicious. We didn't get much chance to have them in Wenzhou because they were quite expensive. I treasured them so much that I didn't share any of them with my roommates, and I only had a little every day. The box of snacks lasted me for 10 days.

At the end of August 1974, our team was ready for the national competition in Suzhou. We took the train to the city. We were put up at a school to stay in. It was the summer holidays, so the schools were empty. We slept on top of desks.

It was the first time I wore a beautifully cut blue nylon leotard with white trim. Previously, we just wore sportswear. We borrowed the leotards from the Hangzhou team. The older girls wore white and red.

During the training session before the National competition, we had the chance to watch the other teams. The Shanghai team had the most competent gymnasts. Their bodies looked so beautiful in their leotards. Their warm-up exercise was so well organized and choreographed. They even had a pianist to accompany them for warm-up exercises. We all watched with envy. Our pianist only accompanied us when we did our floor routines (she was a very good pianist though).

There were photographers taking photos and art students doing sketches of gymnasts everywhere. I saw my photo on the central board along with all the other photos and notices. Mine was taken when I was dismounting from the bars. My dismount, I knew, was the best of all the gymnasts participating. I shot up high in the air before I landed. Another photo of our team was of a girl who was doing her split leap on the beam. We could see her face and her straight legs. It was a beautiful photo.

The competition went for five days. I came fifth all around, fifth on vault and third on bars. I was the one from our team who got the most medals, altogether four medals (one for the team; our team came second after the Shanghai team). One boy who also represented Zhejiang took seven firsts on all the boys' apparatus. He gained seven medals! His name was Lou Yun. He was later selected to the national team in Beijing, became a well-known international top gymnast, and won the gold medal on vault in the 1984 and 1988 Olympics.

After the competition, we went sightseeing. We went to the Tiger Tower, many temples, and the famous Suzhou gardens. We had a great time, and then the team was dismissed. Everyone had to go back to where she or he came from. The glory had ended. The best attention I ever had was gone. I was sad that I had to leave Coach Jiao. I gave her one of my hard-earned medals as a souvenir. She accepted it and also said when I got back to my hometown to give one to my home coach Xia. So I did.

1974 - National Gymnastics competition Zhejiang State team. I was in the middle second row wearing four medals. The boy gymnast on the far right who wore seven medals is LOU YUN. He was selected into the national team in 1978 and eventually won first place in Vault in the 1984 and 1988 Olympics Games. Coach Jiao is in the back row, third from the right.

On the way back to Wenzhou, we stopped at Shanghai. It was my first visit to Shanghai. I was fazed by its tall buildings, neon lights, and the variety of shops. As I mentioned before, I spent all my money in the first 10 days away from home; the small amount of money that was given to us as gymnasts representing the provincial team from the government was spent during the last weeks in Hangzhou and Suzhou. I didn't have any money to buy anything. I had about 20 Jiao left in my pocket. I wanted to buy my grandma some cigarettes because Shanghai had the best cigarettes and Grandma liked them. 20 Jiao was almost nothing. I had to eat as well. I went into a restaurant and bought myself a plate of noodles that cost 18 fen (like 18 cents). I felt that plate of noodles was the best noodles I had ever had as I hadn't eaten all day.

The ship from Shanghai to Wenzhou took 22 hours. From Wenzhou, if you wanted to go anywhere, you either took the ship to Shanghai or the bus to Jinhua where you could catch the train or plane. Wenzhou only had the bus and ship at the time. (Now Wenzhou has everything. The airport was built in 1992, and the train line to Jinhua was completed just a few months before I started to write this book, which was July 1997). I didn't eat at all on the ship. I didn't tell anyone that I had no money. At the time, there was me, the boy from my team, and two coaches from my city on the ship

On the second day on the ship, it was lunchtime. I was lying in my bed and had put a pillow on my stomach. I was very hungry. One of the coaches asked me why I didn't go to lunch. I shook my head and didn't say anything. He asked me if I had run out of money, but I didn't answer. I was ashamed to have to admit that I had no money on me at all. The coach probably guessed it and he gave me 5 Jiao (50 cents) and told me to get some lunch. So, I accepted it - 50 cents allowed me to buy one bowl of noodle soup on the ship. It tasted beautiful.

When I got home, Grandma was a bit disappointed that I did not buy her cigarettes in Shanghai (I had always bought her cigarettes when I went to Hangzhou for competitions in the last two years). She said she had been looking forward to my cigarettes because her quota had finished (cigarettes needed quotas, too). I said I ran out of money. She thought about it and then nodded her head. I felt a bit sad. I felt sad not because she didn't give me enough money; I knew we were always short of money. I felt sad because I didn't get her cigarettes.

After I came back from the national competition, our home team Coach Xia was pregnant with her second child. She couldn't coach anymore, so she put me in charge of the team. She said that as I had learned some new skills and new ways of training from Hangzhou, I could teach my home team. My teammates said my movements and postures were so different from what they were used to before. They were beautiful and more 'professional' - they said.

I was only 13 and I didn't know how to organize the training, of course. There were no coaches in the gym for almost the whole year. Also, my body had started to change. I put on more than 10 kilos in one year. My strength couldn't carry my body weight anymore.

Training without a proper coach was not training, and everybody was slack. A few gymnasts even dropped out.

After the national competition, I started middle school. I was sent to the middle school where Miao was - No. 7 Middle school. It was close to where we lived.

I didn't cope well with the change. On the first day at school, I remember the teacher calling out all the names to mark the roll. When he called my name, I was so nervous that I said yes with a whisper. The teacher didn't hear me. I remember there were a few people in the class who knew me because of my brother (he was well-known at the school both academically and in the dance team.) I was embarrassed because I was the sister of the well-known Miao. I felt some students were staring at me. This made me very uncomfortable and nervous. The teacher called my name again. This time I simply could not speak. He marked me absent that day. I was even more embarrassed after that incident.

Fortunately, that year Wenzhou Sports School was established. I was chosen to go to the sports school, so when a teacher came into my class and said I could go to the other school a week later, I was relieved.

The sports school had grades 3-10, (we only had 10 years of

schooling at that time, Chairman Mao wanted to cut short the school years so the young graduates could go to the countryside to help the peasants). All the students belonged to one or another sports team in Wenzhou, such as basketball, volleyball, table tennis, swimming, athletics, etc. In our class, which was the first year in middle school (equivalent to year seven in Australia), we had all girls; two from gymnastics, one from swimming, and the rest from basketball and the volleyball team. Altogether 14 girls - our class was the smallest.

We went to school in the mornings and trained in the afternoons. We did this six days a week. Obviously, we didn't have enough time to cover all the subjects a normal school would. Hence, we just did the most important subjects like Chinese, Math, Physics, English and Politics. We missed out on subjects such as History, Geography, and Biology.

In primary school, my grades were average. When I got to middle school, I found that most of my classmates were even worse than I was. This boosted my confidence. Doing well in that year's provincial and national competitions had given me a lot of confidence to study. I turned out to be number one in all subjects, except Politics. I hated this subject. It was all about the Communist Party's history. I could never remember when and what the party did during the wars. It seemed far away from me. I was not interested.

We changed our training venue, too. The school built two new gyms - one for gymnastics and one for table tennis. I never liked the new hall. The arrangement of apparatus was different, and I never quite got used to it.

The most important thing was that we didn't have a coach that year. Coach Xia was pregnant. She had put me in charge of the training. I taught younger gymnasts skills and routines that I did for the national competition, and I learned the new routines myself for the older age group for that year.

One afternoon during the training session, I was going to support a girl on bars. I missed her when she dismounted. She fell to the ground and dislocated her elbow. I felt terrible. Luckily, she didn't blame me for that, and we stayed good friends.

By the time the 1975 competition came, I knew I had fallen far behind. We went to Hangzhou again. I was so ashamed that I didn't want to talk to Coach Jiao. I used to be her pride, but now I could hardly run like a gymnast. I was so heavy. When finally, she came up to me, there was no escape. I wished there was a hole in the ground that I could hide myself in. Coach Jiao said to me, *'you must weigh at least 45 kilos now!'* I was so embarrassed that I didn't know what to say. I felt terrible! I don't know what position I finished during that competition. I didn't care.

After that, I thought that was it! That would be the end of my gymnastics career. I told Coach Xia that I wanted to quit. She tried to persuade me into continuing, but I had made up my mind. I thought I was old (15) and fat, and could not possibly do well again in gymnastics. Then she said, *'Stay as a little coach then'.* 'Little coach' means coach assistant. I agreed.

I didn't stay long. I stayed until March 1976, until the time of my life that I mentioned at the beginning of this book, the time when I had to leave my grandma, my school, my gym, my teammates, my coach, my best friends, and my Wenzhou (did you know Wenzhou means 'warm city' in Chinese?) to go to Guangzhou to be with my parents again. I didn't want to go; my parents didn't mean much in my mind then. I was missing my friends in Wenzhou already and I felt I was leaving my life behind, and my happiness, too.

Guangzhou is a Big City

Guangzhou is a big city. It has the same size population as almost the whole of Australia. It is situated in the south of China, two hours by train from Hong Kong. It is also called China's *'South Gate'* and is one of the most modern and commercial cities in China. People in Guangzhou speak Cantonese.

In big cities, people are not as friendly as in small towns. People in Guangzhou looked down upon people from other places. They have a name for them - *'Bei Lao'* (the Northerners) which means people from the north. Because Guangzhou is the biggest city in the far south of China, anyone who is not from there is obviously from the north. That is why they called them *'Bei Lao'*.

Feng and I spoke the Wenzhou dialect. We didn't know Cantonese at all. We didn't understand a word of it. Father and Mother were allowed to have some freedom after 1971. Dad was re-admitted as a member of the Communist Party. They had a meeting, Father said. At the meeting, they announced that how they treated Father during those years was wrong. The torture was a little bit *'overdone'* they said. Father was allowed to participate in party meetings again. Both Mum and Dad returned to the jobs that they did before, as civil engineers. As for Mother, no one said anything until another three years later. One day, a representative from the authority came to our house and apologized to her. He said that she was mistreated during the Cultural Revolution and was a good person. Dad said he felt like giving that person a punch to the nose. But he didn't. Things had been done. What could bring back five years of precious life and replace a twisted heart?! *'Nothing, nothing in the world!'* Dad said.

Many years later, in 1978, the whole of the Cultural Revolution was announced as a mistake in Chinese history. What a tragic mistake; hundreds of thousands were tortured to death, hundreds of thousands killed themselves to escape the torture, and hundreds of thousands of families were destroyed.

Our parents didn't say anything about what had happened to them to Feng and me at all. They didn't ask us about our life in Wenzhou either. They just worked.

We arrived at our parents' place. It was a nine square metre room in the corner of the company canteen - the company both Mum and Dad worked for, the Guangdong Transportation Bureau.

Father and Mother came back to Guangzhou from the camp in 1973. The company gave them that room. At the age of 40 and 44, Mum and Dad had just this tiny room where they could settle with no kitchen, no bathroom, just a room of nine square meters. Mum had a portable stove that could be taken in and out of the room. When she had to cook, she would have to carry it out and cook in the corner of the canteen outside her room. The toilets were office toilets upstairs.

When I walked into the room, I saw two big timber pillars supporting the ceiling on one side of the room - next door was a building site. The pillars were there to support the ceiling from falling when the machine was hammering concrete stumps down into the ground outside the window.

Inside the room, there was a double bed, a chest of drawers, a desk, and a chair. That's all Mum and Dad had.

Because Mum and Dad had me and Feng back, the company gave them another even smaller room upstairs outside an office. Actually, it was part of the hallway, only fenced with some timber in the corner and Mum and Dad slept on top of a big table in that room. Grandma, Feng, and I all slept in the double bed downstairs. Fortunately, we were all short. We slept sideways on the bed, with our heads banging against the wall and our legs sticking out of the edge of the bed. Grandma stayed for a few months. She would have liked to stay with us longer, but she was worrying about Miao who had been left alone in Wenzhou.

I was shocked and disappointed by the condition Mum and Dad were living in. Before we came, we thought Guangzhou was such a big and modern city that the living standard in Guangzhou would be a lot better than in Wenzhou, but it was not. It was a lot worse than Grandma's place. We actually had no place to sit down in the room but had to sit outside in the canteen.

Feng and I missed our friends in Wenzhou terribly. We didn't know anybody in Guangzhou. We didn't know the streets. We didn't know the language. We were like the blind and deaf, and Mum went to work the second day.

Feng was put into school soon after we arrived in Guangzhou. He was in grade two in the No. 10 Middle School near our home. I stayed at home for nearly six months. I'd started school a year earlier than average children. When I transferred to Guangzhou, Mum and Dad decided that I would repeat one year, so I would start the next school year, which was in September.

Father came back a few days later. The morning when he arrived home, no one was home except me. I remember that scene very clearly. He walked into the room. I stood up, with a book in my hand. I called him *'Ba'*, and he smiled and looked at me. We both looked at each other but didn't know what to say. Then he asked me where Feng was, in Mandarin. I answered him back in the Wenzhou dialect. I just assumed that he knew the Wenzhou dialect. He was puzzled. He didn't understand what I said, so I repeated it in Mandarin. I felt embarrassed to speak Mandarin because it was not my mother tongue.

I could never forget this first meeting with my father after our 10 years of separation. He was thin and dark, dressed in a grey jacket and with his back slightly bent. He looked very old to me. He had a black bag in his hand. I liked his smile, however in the years that followed that smile didn't come easily. I worked so very hard to see that smile on his face.

I had nothing to do during those six months at home. Mum's company had a library, so I borrowed lots of novels. I read a novel a day. Most of them were revolutionary novels and I forgot about the first one when I picked up the second one. It was just a matter of killing time.

However, Mum and Dad were not happy. Not only did they never ask us about our lives in Wenzhou, but they criticized Feng and me for whatever we did. We were just not right whichever way they looked at us (horizontally or vertically, that's what we say). Of course, we were strangers living under the same roof. They didn't know us, nor did we know them.

'Why', hundreds and hundreds of times I asked in my heart, *'why on earth did you want us back if we were creatures that you dislike so much? Why on earth were we born at all?'* I couldn't find the answer. I was looking for the answer almost all my life after that.

Of course, I didn't know what had happened to them during those 10 years of the Cultural Revolution. I didn't understand what the Cultural Revolution was at all. All I saw was the constant unhappiness and disapproval of my parents.

After Grandma left, obviously it was not a good idea that Feng and I slept in one double bed, so Mum and Dad moved downstairs. They had their double bed back. I slept upstairs in the tiny room on top of the big table. Feng was put outside Mum's room, in the corner of the big, tall, and open canteen that had a courtyard with no roof. Two timber benches and two slices of timber, one hay sheet, and a net - that was Feng's bed. He could not go to bed until the TV, which was in the canteen for everyone to watch during the evening, finished, and he had to get up in the morning before people turned up for breakfast. He had to undo his bed in the morning and put things away, then he set up his bed every night in the evening. In the winter, the northern wind cut through people's bones, but Feng slept with a single quilt. You could see his net moving in the wind, and Mum and Dad didn't even care. They simply didn't notice! Feng kept his mouth shut. He refused to talk, even to me. My heart was twisting around just watching him suffer.

I felt like I was in this deep, dark tunnel where I could not see a single light. It was cold and wet and windy there. I saw myself there with Feng a few metres away from me. Apart from the horror, mystery, and misery, I felt I was responsible for Feng. I needed to comfort him. He was still so young. He didn't understand anything, but he was suffering.

I held on to these feelings as there was no one to turn to. No one would understand. No one in this world, I thought.

We lived just one street away from the Pearl River. I often

wandered around on the bank, thinking, and thinking. A couple of times, I walked up the big bridge and stood on the edge. With all these people around me on the bikes or just walking, and those neon lights on both sides of the bank flashing, I looked down to the river and thought, *'what would it be like if I jumped off this bridge? What is it like down there under the water? I'd be kicking and holding my breath for a while,'* I thought. *'And then I'd be choking. I don't like the feeling of choking. It is not a nice way to die.'* Would there be a better way? I often wondered.

Despite having all these thoughts, I had to look after the daily housework for the family. Mum and Dad were working, and Feng was at school. Only I had plenty of time. Endless time. The market was not far from where we lived. Every afternoon I had to go to the empty market, queuing up with all those old ladies for whatever would arrive, who knows what time later. I didn't speak the dialect. Sometimes, people would push in front of me and I didn't know what to say. If I said something in the Wenzhou dialect or in Mandarin, it would make matters worse. Other times, I would queue up at the wrong window. When the goods arrived at another window, we would fight to get to that window first, which ended up in chaos, of course. No one knew when and where and what we were going to get. Sometimes you waited for hours, and nothing would come. I hated that market. I hated those ladies around me. I hated Guangzhou. I hated its rude and unkind people, and I hated my parents, too.

I spent hours and hours writing letters to friends in Wenzhou. Every day, my biggest moment was when the postman arrived. All my life was put on hold waiting for those letters. If I had mail that day, I was happy for the rest of the day until Mum and Dad finished work. If I didn't have any mail, I'd put all my hope on tomorrow. Every day was like this. Expecting and waiting.

In the evenings before I went to bed, I would sit in my bed with my legs crossed, palms together in front of my heart and I prayed. I was not brought up in a religious family, but I was desperate. I prayed very hard every day. *'Dear God,'* I would say, *'please use your power to free me. Send me and Feng back to Wenzhou and bring me back my friends.'* That's all I wanted. *'I will go back to Wenzhou one day,'* I swore to myself.

In the meantime, Feng was not doing well at school. He'd come home with bruises and cuts. We asked him why. He said he fought with everyone at school who called him names (the *'northerners'*). He was only small, but he said in the end everyone at the school was frightened of him.

I noticed he had a tattoo of a sort of symbol on his lower arm one day. It was a black triangle. I asked him what it was. He wouldn't tell me. I asked him how he did it. He said he used a knife and ink. I was scared. *'Dear god,'* I prayed, *'please help me!'* I worried about him a lot. Mum and Dad didn't understand him, of course. They just blamed him - blamed us. Everything we did was never good enough. *'Whatever we do, God!'* I said to myself, *'why are they so merciless, so cruel? Haven't they hearts?'*

They said they were critical because they wanted us to be good. *'Wanted us to be good!'* I thought, *'You are lucky that we didn't end up in the streets or killing ourselves.'*

Actually, Feng almost did.

One day, Feng didn't come back from school. We ate our dinner in silence (we always ate our dinner in silence). He didn't come back the second night. We went to his school. The teacher said he hadn't turned up for school. We went to one of his good friend's homes (the only one we knew of) who said he hadn't seen him. Mum and Dad went out into the streets to look for him, but he was nowhere to be seen.

On the third morning, Dad found him. He found him outside the railway station. Feng said he had borrowed some money from friends and was going to take the train to Wenzhou that afternoon if Dad hadn't found him that morning.

Nothing was said or discussed about Feng's attempt to run away.

Our lives went back to normal. I continued my prayers every night, begging God to send Feng and me back to Grandma.

Mum and Dad tried to get me back to gymnastics again. Maybe they noticed I was very unhappy. One day, Father took me to the Guangzhou City gymnastic team. I had a letter from Coach Xia when I left Wenzhou; Dad gave the letter to the head coach. She examined me from head to toe after reading the letter. I think she didn't believe whatever Coach Xia had said in the letter. I was very embarrassed because I knew I was too fat to be a gymnast again, but she let me try a few things. I remember I got on the bars. When I finished, I could see that she and some of the gymnasts who were watching were quite surprised that such a fat girl could do things on bars at such a high standard, but she was still concerned about my weight. I just wanted to get out of there as quickly as possible. She asked me if I wanted to stay as an assistant coach. I said I would let her know later and I went home.

I didn't want to think of gymnastics again! Mum and Dad couldn't understand why I didn't want to continue with gymnastics because when I was in the Wenzhou gymnastic team, they didn't want me to continue - they thought it was too dangerous. I had ignored their disapproval and did what I wanted to do. Now they wanted me to pick up gymnastics again and I refused. *'What's the matter with this girl?'* they must have thought.

I started school in September. Mum went to the Education Bureau and found me a middle school that was a 45-minute walk from where we lived. She didn't want me just to go to an ordinary school nearby. The school took me because of my gymnastic background. The school was known as one with a good gymnastic history. But when I went there, their gymnastics team had long disappeared. It was only in their history from before the Cultural Revolution.

No. 2 Middle School

So, I went to No. 2 Middle School in Guangzhou, which is situated under the foot of the well-known mountain (hill) called Yue-Xiou. The symbol of Guangzhou, the Five Goats statue, is there.

On the first day of school, we were having a big assembly. The school had over 2000 students from what we called middle one to high two, similar to grades 7 to 10 here. Most students in my class, which was high one, were continuing students from middle two at the same school. I was new.

We lined up in the big asphalt playground. Our teacher was assigning some class positions, such as academic representatives, sports representatives, math representatives, etc. to the students she knew. There was one position left that she couldn't find a suitable person to fill in. She looked at me (because I was short and was at the front of the line) and asked me if I would like to be the physics representative. I didn't say no. I didn't say yes either. I didn't know what to say because she asked me in Cantonese which I wasn't sure if I understood. She took my silence as yes (that's our Chinese way because people assume silence as being shy and too humble to say yes). So, I became the physics representative for that year. The subject representatives were students who were good (supposed to be the best) at those subjects. She didn't even know me. *'She must have run out of people,'* I thought.

All subject representatives automatically became what we called class leaders (plus the monitor). We often stayed after school to have meetings to discuss issues relating to class tasks such as cleaning up the classroom and the schoolyard and what to put on the class board, which was at the back of the classroom and needed to be changed every week. There were about 10 class leaders in my class. Among these 10 students, most of them were not originally from Guangzhou. They were the kids from the armies whose parents came down from other cities. So we spoke Mandarin to each other. This removed great pressure from my head because, at the time, I hated Cantonese so much that I refused to learn it. I didn't want anything to do with it.

We became very good friends for the rest of the two years in high school. Girls and boys didn't speak to each other at schools in those days, but we class leaders got along very well. Our friendships lasted many, many years - even after we finished high school and went to different universities.

I still didn't understand Cantonese after six months in Guangzhou. Teachers taught lessons in Cantonese in most schools in Guangzhou in those days. Even with the Chinese classes, our teacher would explain notes in Cantonese. Most times I sat there, watching the teacher walking from the left to the right and from the right to the left at the front, trying to understand what he or she was saying. My mind often wandered away.

One day, the chemistry teacher walked past me as he was teaching. He saw the textbook on my desk, which was different from the ones of other students - I had brought it from Wenzhou. At that time, every province had its own curriculum. Therefore, all the textbooks were different from each other. The teacher picked mine up and flipped through it. He asked me where I was up to. I pointed to the chapter I was up to before I came to Guangzhou (which was when I was at the sports school; we were far behind). He didn't say anything. At the end of the term, when I got my exam paper back, my score was 98 out of 100. I didn't finish all the exercises on the paper. I only did what I was taught and knew that term. I was so grateful to him. Thank you, Mr Yang. I will never forget you.

Another incident I remember also related to Mr Yang. He gave us an assignment that he later would select a few students to do a presentation in front of the class. Presentations did not happen very often in Chinese schools. The assignment was about how steel was refined from ore. I prepared my assignment carefully because I didn't want to embarrass myself in front of the class just in case I was picked. Mr Yang saw my preparation and he picked me! The other girl he selected was *'top of the class'* - our academic representative in all areas. After the presentation, some students told me that they now understood how steel was refined from ore because of my presentation - not even from Mr Yang. I was very pleased with myself and thankful to Mr Yang for giving me the opportunity.

Our class leaders often organized weekend outings (without the class of course). Once, we rode our bicycles to White Clouds Mountain, which was one and a half hours away from the city. Another time, we went to a friend's home to make dumplings and just talk. I really enjoyed their company. Among us, there was a girl whose name was Lengxi, which meant *'Look down upon the West'*, which we thought her parents must have changed during the Cultural Revolution. And a boy whose name was Weidong, which meant *'protect the East'*. We often joked about the two of them, saying the two of them were born a pair. We didn't know that later on they'd become lovers, and I didn't know that, many years later, Weidong would become the first boy whom I'd have a crush on.

Lengxi and I became good friends. She was tall and good-looking, and I liked her immediately after I saw her. She was with the school dancing team then. I watched her solo dance at one of the school performances - the name of the dance was *'The girl who looks after the pigs.'* It was about a high school graduate who was sent to the remote country to breed pigs, and the expression of the dance was how happy she was in the pigsty. Lengxi danced well, but not as good as my brother, of course. She looked very happy in the dance. She spoke Mandarin, of course. Her parents were with the army, and her Cantonese was awful, but that didn't worry me at all since I decided that I was never going to learn Cantonese. I asked Lengxi to be my Communist Youth League sponsor.

The Communist Youth League was an association one step higher than the Red Guards (another step further and you would become a Communist Party member). Not everyone could become a member. You had to be good in all areas to be able to apply for membership, and you needed to find a member to introduce you. I wanted to become a member, not because I was interested in the communist theory or policy or anything, but simply because it was a symbol of outstanding achievement. I wrote an application letter and gave it to Lengxi. She had never introduced anyone to become a member before, she said, and she was pleased with my request.

Middle school passed quickly. My results were very good although I didn't understand the teachers for almost half of the year. The education standard in Zhejiang province was higher than in Guangdong, but I didn't even put much effort into my studies. Lengxi admired my achievement. She always wanted to do well in studying but somehow, she never got good results, so she was not very happy about that.

The year was 1976, the year a big event happened in Chinese

history - Chairman Mao died. The chairman of the Communist Party since 1949, who controlled China for 27 years, was dead at the age of 87. He was still in the position when he died. Almost everyone in China participated in his funeral in one way or another. I remember our whole school was designated to be at Pearl Square near the Pearl River (near the bridge I wanted to jump off) to listen to the funeral, which was held in Beijing via big loudspeakers. We stood in lines for hours. A few classmates cried, one girl fainted. We were not sure if it was from sadness or because she stood there for too long.

China changed dramatically after Mao's death. First of all, the great Cultural Revolution was pronounced as a mistake. Those people who were put into the Cowsheds and labelled as anti-revolutionists returned to work. Their salaries for all those years were given back. High school graduates who were sent to those remote country areas started to return to their home cities. It was then that *'wounded literature'* was born. Those stories were about the lives of the high school graduates who were sent to remote countryside. I read a lot of them. Compared with their lives, my life was nothing, I thought.

In 1977, all the universities in China started to take students fairly, according to their exam results. During the 10-year period of the Cultural Revolution, universities only took students who were chosen by the Party. The Communist Party had the total authority to decide who would attend which universities and what he or she would study.

The first national exam for universities after the Cultural Revolution took place in the spring of 1978. My brother Miao went for the exam that year. Unfortunately, that year, students had to select which universities they would like to attend before they knew their scores. Miao chose three good ones that needed higher marks to get in. His score wasn't high enough and there wasn't a second chance to choose other colleges, so he missed out on going to university.

My school started a new system. For the final year in high school, we formed what we called key classes. Only the best students were selected to be in these key classes. There were two types of key classes - one for students who were going to pursue art degrees when they went on to university, the other for those who wanted to do their science or engineering degrees. We were given the choice of going to either one. Because I went to a sports school in Wenzhou, I missed out on a lot of subjects, such as history and geography, which would be examined leading to an art degree. Also, at that time, only those students who were not good at Maths, Physics, and Chemistry were going to the class that led to arts degrees, which were looked down upon. My parents always wanted me to become an engineer. So, I went into the scientific key class without a thought. Lengxi chose the arts strand. Altogether, there were four key classes out of almost 17 classes in my final year. I was in key class Number Three. We were given the best teachers at the school. Number Two Middle School was, before the Cultural Revolution, one of the top schools in Guangzhou. The teachers were almost the best in town. Looking back, I was lucky that Mum bothered to spend some time finding me a good school. I have been very grateful for that.

Our time was filled with tons of homework. The exercise paper printed in blue ink was never-ending. I wasn't very keen on studying and didn't care whether or not I went to university. In fact, I had not given any thought to my future. I was still miserable just being in Guangzhou; being with my parents. I couldn't see anything in my future.

Mum and Dad pushed me as hard as they could. After dinner, I had to go to my room upstairs to study, every night.

I was not allowed to go out or watch any TV.

Towards the end, I was happy that I had that tiny room - at least it was my space. I could do anything I wanted (except swing a cat!). While Mum and Dad thought I was studying hard, I was actually reading novels. I read one of the most famous four-series novels called *'The Red Mansions'*, and it became one of my favourite Chinese novels. It was a love story with a very sad ending (the girl died). There were films and TV series written about it. One night, Dad came up to check up on me (I thought), and I quickly put the novel under the quilt on my bed, but the book was so thick you could see the lump under the quilt. I was so scared that Dad would notice it, but he didn't - or he pretended that he didn't. He gave me a book which was the collection of 1978's spring exams on three important subjects: Math, Physics and Chemistry. The 1978 spring exam was the only one when every province created their own paper. Therefore, the exams were different from one province to another.

I did do those exercises. Sometimes I found myself enjoying solving those problems in Math or Physics. Besides, what else could I do after school? I wasn't allowed to go out. I worked hard towards the end. I didn't want to upset Mum and Dad; add another episode to the already unhappy situation.

In July 1978, the big day came. My parents were more anxious than I was. They got up early, prepared breakfast for me, and then hurried me on my way to the exam site. I was assigned to another school for the exams. All the seats were carefully arranged so we didn't sit next to a student we knew to prevent us from cheating. The exams took three days, including the subjects of Math, Chinese, Physics, Chemistry, Politics, and English. Two exams on one day - one in the morning, one in the afternoon. The English score didn't count towards the total score that year because a lot of schools stopped English classes during the Cultural Revolution. I didn't think I did well. I was glad that the pressure and anxiety was over.

Waiting for the exam results was like waiting for the final judgment of my fate. I wasn't that anxious, but Mum and Dad were very nervous.

One day, about a month later, as I was sitting on a chair in Mum's company canteen (that was where I usually sat), a few of my schoolmates ran in and shouted to me:

'You are in! You are in!' they said.

'Really? What's my score?' I asked.

'Come to school with us, you'll see,' they said.

So I went to school. It was in the middle of the summer holidays and school was very quiet, with not a single person in sight. All I remembered was in the classroom where we last attended there was this blackboard. On the blackboard, there were 18 names with the scores beside them. My name was there, and the score was 334. Those were the names of students who passed the entry line for entering universities that year. Out of over one thousand graduates, only 18 got in. I was one of the only two girls, and Weidong got in, too - his score was 270 and something. Lengxi missed out.

In China, to get into universities, the system worked like this: according to the number of the intake of all the universities and the number of participants in the exams, the authority would set three 'entry' scores. One for key universities, one for normal universities, and one for colleges. In my year, the score for entering key universities was 330. The score for colleges was 260. I was definitely going to a university. That put my heart at ease. *I'm leaving home! Leaving this unhappy place. All will be fine. My life will start again.*

When the time came that I had to choose a university and a major, I was very confused. I couldn't think. I was 17 - no, not even 17 yet, one month away. I hadn't given any thought to what I was going to do for a career. My future seemed far away. All my thoughts for the past two years were about the unhappy state I was in. I stopped growing; I refused to grow. I had been wishing that I had never gone to Guangzhou.

Actually, Psychology came across my mind a couple of times, but that was an arts degree. I took the road that would lead to a Science or Engineering degree because I missed some subjects in sports school, so I couldn't do what I thought I was interested in. When Mum and Dad chose the major for me after numerous sleepless nights, I didn't care what it was.

I was admitted to the Department of Radio Technology at South-China University of Technology (SCUT) which was situated on the south side of Guangzhou city, about one and a half hours away by bus. Electronics was a hot area to get into at that time. Radio Technology was one of the top departments at SCUT. Mum and Dad didn't want me to go to another city to study. I was afraid to go to another city to start all over again after I had been through the experience in Guangzhou.

So, we settled for the Department of Radio Engineering at SCUT.

What a relief. That stressful time was over. I felt light and free again.

Miao also participated in this year's exam, but he failed to reach the entry score. He didn't want to go to university anymore after two attempts.

Beginning University

Just a few weeks after my 17th birthday, Mum and Dad accompanied me to the South-China University of Technology. It was enrolment day. All new students were asked to go to a stadium to be greeted by administrative staff and to listen to the speech given by the vice-chancellor. The hall was packed with thousands of new students from all over China and their luggage and parents. After the speech, we were sent to the departments that we applied for to enrol there. We also found out where our rooms were.

South-China University of Technology has a large campus. There were altogether about 20,000 students, lecturers, and admin staff on the campus, with more than 20 departments. Every department had its own building with countless lecture theatres and dormitories.

The university has two lakes; one called East Lake, and the other West Lake. It is quite a beautiful university.

The girls' dormitories were on the west side of East Lake; the boys' dorms were on the east side. I was assigned to West Two girls' dorm. My room number was 305, which was on the 3rd floor (the top floor).

Mum and Dad helped me with my luggage - a quilt, a net for keeping mosquitoes out, some linen, and clothes. Our room had four double bunk beds, two on each side as you walked into the room. There were seven girls. At the front of the room near the window were seven small desks all cramped up against each other with one desk and a stool each.

When I arrived, almost all the girls had already set up their beds. I put my quilt on an empty bed, which was at the lower front on the left-hand side. Mum immediately asked around if there was anyone from Zhejiang Province. She probably sensed that I didn't feel like I belonged to Guangzhou. She found there was one in the room opposite us - room 306. The girl was from a place not far from Hangzhou - the capital city of Zhejiang province, where I had my gymnastics competitions. Mum was happy for me because she thought at least there was someone from my 'hometown'. Her name was Jianping. I didn't care that much at the time. Everything was new to me, and I was curious, but still shy.

The day was Sunday. Mum and Dad went back home after they saw me settle into my room. They wouldn't be seeing me until the next Saturday, which didn't worry me at all.

Among the seven of us, five were high school graduates from that year, aged 17 or 18. One was 19, and the other was our big sister, Zhixing, who was 25. She was the one who belonged to the wounded generation. She was sent to Hainan Island to look after rubber trees for eight years after graduating from high school. We all admired her courage and perseverance for participating in the exams and for passing the very strict selection criteria to be there. 25 was the age limit to take the exams for universities. Above 25, you were not allowed to take the entry exam anymore.

There were four people in our room from Guangdong province - me and the big sister from Guangzhou, one from the campus as her parents were lecturers at SCUT, and another girl from the country in Guangdong province. The other three people were from other provinces including Shan'Xi, Sichuang, and Guangxi.

I set up my bed and sat on the edge, chatting away with my roommates. Later, we bought some canteen dockets and went to the canteen to have our dinner.

Our canteen was at the back of the boys' dorm on the east side. We were assigned to this canteen and couldn't go to any other ones, although some were closer to us. We all had a big bowl and a spoon. We didn't use chopsticks because there was only one dish anyway, which was usually on top of rice. We didn't need chopsticks to pick up anything as it was faster to eat with a spoon.

For the first term, everybody was given the same amount of rice and a dish to go with it - usually a piece of fatty meat and some vegetables. There was no choice of food or the amount of food. The boys didn't have enough to eat; the girls had to chuck some rice out because it was too much. At the end of the term, we'd had enough. We wanted to be able to at least choose the amount of food we ate. The year was 1977. Students (who were only half a year earlier than us, most of them were from the wounded generation and much older than us), organized a demonstration.

We marched to the school administration building and demanded better quality food and freedom of choice in the canteens as well as choosing the quantity of rice. I remember one cartoon drawing outside the administrative building showed a student who came into the university with a big belly and when he graduated, he was as thin as a skeleton, indicating that the university didn't provide him with enough food. I thought the cartoon was very clever and funny.

Things started to improve immediately. We had more dishes to choose from and a choice of the amount too. We had the flexibility to choose which canteen we wanted to go to and how much money we wanted to spend, depending on how many dishes we wanted to buy. This brought competition between canteens. They had to improve the quality of their food; otherwise, there would be fewer people going there.

We were very happy with our victory!

Accommodation at universities in China was free, but the food was at our own expense. Some of us were given subsidies from the government according to how much income our parents earned. We all had to fill in a form showing how many family members there were and how much income our parents earned. The class leaders discussed and decided who should get what grade subsidies.

Mine was 16 Yuan per month, which was about 3 Australian dollars. But 16 Yuan at the time almost covered my food for the month. I didn't have to ask my parents to give me money for food. If there is anything I am grateful to the Chinese government for, then that is the free university education and free accommodation.

We had five subjects in the first term; all were compulsory. Actually, in China, almost all subjects at universities were compulsory except in the fourth year when we had the choice of one or two elective subjects, and a second foreign language between German and Japanese to pick from.

My results for the first term were quite good, although I found the subjects were very boring. I got 98 for high Math; others were between 75 and 90, so I was happy about the scores.

All the girls in my room studied very hard. Apart from going to lectures, eating and sleeping, they spent every spare moment on their studies, day after day, including weekends.

I felt the pressure and I was not used to it. I was still thinking of high school. When I finished the homework we were given, all my other time belonged to me. I wanted to do something else, but I was alone. I couldn't ask anyone to give up their precious time to talk to me or go out with me. Besides, there was nothing to do and nowhere to go anyway. Our university was situated on the outskirts of Guangzhou, so there were no shops or cinemas around.

I remember one afternoon when we had no lectures; I was sitting on my bed feeling bored. I couldn't read any more of those textbooks. While I was watching the other six girls sitting there silently reading or doing exercises, I thought to myself, *'are these people mad?'* How could they spend their whole lives burying themselves in those boring books? Was this necessary?

I was still missing my friends in Wenzhou and spent a lot of time writing letters and waiting for letters. Receiving mail was still the most important moment in my life. I still kept in touch with my gymnastic mates, my brother Miao, and of course my best friend Wei.

At the end of the second term (first year had ended), I asked Mum and Dad if they would allow me to go to Wenzhou for a visit. To my surprise, they agreed without hesitation. For the first time, I felt they gave me a positive answer when I asked them for something.

Later when I asked them why, they said they were happy that I got into university. Allowing me to visit Grandma and Wenzhou was a bonus for what I had achieved. I was so moved that I was almost in tears, and I was excited - very excited. The dream had come true. I had said that one day I would go back to Wenzhou again; now the day had come! It didn't matter if it was just a visit or whatever, as long as I was going back. I had been away for three years! Such a long, long three years. Things I had experienced in those three years! From an active and innocent young girl, I grew to be an introverted and thoughtful lady. I felt I had lived through two lives.

I organized the trip with Jianping - the girl who came from Zhejiang province, and a few other students from other departments who were also from the same province. We bought the train tickets together and off we went. It was the summer holidays of 1979.

The trip on the train was very pleasant. We all had seats because Guangzhou was the beginning of the trip. The five of us were talking and laughing all the way, despite the crowded and dirty conditions on the train.

Jianping got off before me. I had to sit for another three hours to get to Jinhua where I would change to a bus for Wenzhou. Buses for Wenzhou only left in the mornings and our train arrived at Jinhua in the afternoon.

Fortunately, among us, there was a boy from Jinhua who was very friendly with me. He helped me find a cheap hotel to stay at overnight and get a bus ticket for the second day.

The boy saw me off at the bus station and asked me to write to him saying when I was coming back so he could buy the train ticket for me, and we could go back to Guangzhou together. I didn't answer. My intuition told me that this boy wanted to be friends with me and for some reason I was scared. It was not that I disliked him. I didn't know why. It was safer to keep a distance. I had already made up my mind that I was not going to contact him on my way back to Guangzhou.

Return to Wenzhou

1979 - Reunited with Grandma and Miao after leaving them for Guangzhou three years earlier.

The bus took me through the familiar, winding roads on the cliffs of the mountains. Under the cliffs, there were rivers following the same winding curves. The scenery was beautiful.

The road from Wenzhou to Jinhua was quite dangerous. There were often landslides or crashes in the tunnels because of the rain, but to me, the danger added to the beauty of the scenery. I looked outside the window to the misty mountains, feeling this joy and pleasure inside me.

When the bus drove into the Wenzhou bus station, my heart started to beat very fast. I put my hand on my chest to calm myself down.

Oh, Wenzhou, my dream, my memories! Have you changed much since I left three years ago?

Wei and Miao met me at the station. When I saw Wei, I immediately noticed that she had lost a lot of weight. She was already thin, but now she was thinner! *'What happened?'* I asked myself. I knew through her letters that she was going out with a boy from the factory where she worked as a draftsperson and that her mother disapproved of their relationship. Was it because of this that she lost weight?

I didn't ask her. We hadn't been together for three years. In those three years, she dropped out of school because her mother didn't want her to go to the remote countryside when she finished high school. In those years, according to Mao's policy, high school graduates would be automatically sent to the remote countryside. Dropping out of schooling was one way of avoiding being sent away.

Miao was thin too. Since he failed to go to university, he had been struggling to find a proper career. Although our parents didn't like what he chose, he joined the Wenzhou Dance and Play Assembly and became a dancer and actor. He had loved dancing all his life. Dancing and acting were, in our parents' eyes, not a proper career, they would say. *'One isn't paid well through dancing or acting unless he becomes very famous.'* Our parents constantly reminded Miao of this in their letters. Besides, the Wenzhou Dance and Play Assembly had just been established and was struggling to survive itself. Miao was lost and didn't know what to do. He was a career-driven person, but at the time, he couldn't see his future.

We went home, Grandma's home.

Grandma was very happy to see me. She cut up a watermelon

immediately and we all had a few pieces. It was July - right in the middle of summer.

Wei and I went to the photo studio again to mark our reunion after three years apart. I visited Wenzhou during the university summer holiday in 1979.

Wei stayed with us for dinner that night. After dinner, she took me to her home to see her parents. Wei's parents knew me very well. I was in and out of their home all the time when we were in primary school. I even called them Mum and Dad, instead of, what people normally call their friends' parents, Wei's Mum, or Wei's Dad.

I gave them the presents I bought in Guangzhou. Her Mum and Dad asked me to stay at their place that night, but I didn't. It was the first night back home after three years; I wanted to stay with Grandma and Miao. I wanted to share a bed with Grandma again.

That night, Grandma, Miao and I talked and talked until 2:00 o'clock in the morning, and that night I wrote my first diary entry in a beautiful notebook that Lengxi gave me as a present because I was admitted into university.

I was excited and very emotional. I had been waiting for three years for this moment. In all that time in Guangzhou, I only had one wish. I wished that I could return to Wenzhou and stay with Grandma again. I didn't like Guangzhou at all. My parents were too strict and cold, and I was not used to them. And now this was happening. I felt I was living in my dreams.

I could not express to Grandma and Miao, or Wei, the feelings that I had been suppressing for three years. I didn't know how to. Actually, I had never learned to express my emotions to anyone - partly because of the Chinese culture, partly because of my upbringing. But somehow, the bottled-up feelings had to have an outlet, so I started to write in my diary.

In the following three years at the university, my diary became a good friend. Whenever I felt sad, lonely, or angry, I just wrote them down in my diary. To a certain extent, my diary kept me alive.

I spent a whole month in Wenzhou, despite my mother's letters that urged me to go back to Guangzhou. I stayed until the very last day of the summer holidays - until I couldn't stay a day longer.

During that month, there were many get-togethers with my gymnastics teammates and my primary schoolmates. We went to the *'River Heart Island'* where Wei and I went on our first day trip away from Wenzhou alone and took some memorable photos.

Almost all my gymnastics teammates had stopped gymnastics, one by one, after I left. They all grew older. Some wanted to put effort into their studies now that there was a chance to get into university, and others started working. Coach Xia was transferred to a middle school to teach physical education. She wasn't happy, but that was the arrangement. I didn't understand why.

I went back to the gymnasium where I trained. The gymnasium was almost the same except the equipment looked older, and the atmosphere had a run-down feeling. I was sad. Actually, the Wenzhou gymnastic team never reached the stage of when it was in its beginning years.

I also spent a lot of evenings watching Miao's performances in theatres. I had the privilege of going backstage and watching the actors doing make-up and putting on dresses. I really enjoyed watching them backstage on those evenings. Miao was not very good at plays, I thought. He didn't have a good voice and he only played minor parts.

On the morning of the 31st of August 1979, it was time for me to leave Wenzhou again. Grandma, Miao, Wei, and a few of my gymnastics friends saw me off at Wenzhou bus station. I told Grandma that I had a friend in Jinhua who would arrange the train ticket for me, so she didn't have to worry.

As the bus slowly drove out of the station and left my dear Grandma, my brother, and my other friends behind, my heart became heavier and heavier. 'When would I see them again?' I asked myself. I didn't know. I couldn't see that time, anyway.

The bus arrived at Jinhua at about 3 o'clock in the afternoon. The next train to Guangzhou would arrive at 5:30 pm, so I slowly dragged myself to the ticket office at the train station.

There were long queues at every ticket window. I stood at the end of one queue and as the queue moved slowly forward, so did the clock. It was almost 5 o'clock and the office would close at 5:00 o'clock. My mind raced fast. *'No!'* I thought to myself. If I did not catch this train, I would be late for school, and I'd have to find somewhere to stay that night. I had no idea where I could find a hotel and I wasn't sure if I had enough money! I took a deep breath and walked up to the top of the queue with my luggage. A few people looked at me suspiciously, but I didn't care. I walked up to the second person from the widow, explained my situation, and told him how much trouble I would get myself into if I don't get this ticket.

While he was still half-thinking and hesitating, I slipped in the front and bought the ticket. A few minutes later, the window closed. I thought to myself, *'I should have contacted that boy. Why didn't I?'*

I don't know how I got on that train. There were people everywhere. They were trying to climb through windows or were pulling other people out so they themselves could get on. I used all my energy to push myself in. I was almost wet inside and out with sweat as I stood beside the toilet door with my bags at my feet.

There was no limit to how many people could travel on trains in those days in China. Only people from the beginning station would have seats. All the passengers at intermediate stations would have to stand and had to wait for people to get off before they could have a seat. Sometimes they would have to stand for the whole trip, whether it was 10 hours or 35 hours.

On the train I boarded, people occupied every space where you could put a foot in. Back-to-back or face-to-face, it didn't matter. Train services like delivering water and food had completely stopped because it was impossible to get through. People were even unable to go to the toilet and there were people smoking and spitting everywhere.

'At least I got on, and I won't be late for school now,' I told myself and closed my eyes. I was going to stand there for 32 hours!

A few hours later, as I opened my eyes, I saw a young man who had managed to get himself to the end of the compartment to get some water. He saw me and asked me if I was a student going to Guangzhou. I nodded my head. He said, *'Follow me.'* So I followed him. He helped me with my bags. It turned out that he was from Shanghai - the station of origin, so he had a seat. A passenger next to him got off in Jinhua, so he saved the seat. He said he saved the seat for students as he knew there would be many along the way. I felt what he did was not fair to other passengers, but I sat down anyway, too tired to think what was fair and what was not.

Over the journey, I found out that this young man was a student from the Guangzhou Foreign Language Institute, majoring in English. His home was in Shanghai.

The trip became quite enjoyable since I had a seat and company. We took turns getting some food at the stations when the train stopped. Sometimes we just had to reach out from the window as there were a lot of people selling food at each stop. They would come to the windows. At the end of the trip, he left me with his name and address. He asked me to contact him, but I didn't. Again, there was a fear. I didn't know why.

The train arrived at Guangzhou station at 10:30 in the evening on the second day. Mum and Dad met me at the station. I could see from Dad's face that he was not happy. I knew he was not happy because I stayed for too long in Wenzhou, but I didn't care too much.

I went to the university on the second day - September 2nd,1979. School started on the 3rd.

On the 4th of September, I wrote in my diary: *'It is my 18th birthday. I am left alone again. No one has wished me Happy Birthday.'*

South China University of Technology

We had to have military training for three weeks at the beginning of the second year of university. We learned shooting and throwing a hand grenade as well as ground exercises - like how to move fast while we were on our stomachs so as not to be seen by enemies. I was very interested in this training. It was much more interesting than dull textbooks, I thought.

Before we shot with real rifles at the end of the training, we did the exercise *'aiming'* first. It was summer. We were required to lie on the ground, aiming at the target for hours until our eyes became very sore. While I was aiming, I chatted with the soldiers. There were three soldiers who came to our university to train us. I found out that the soldier who trained our class fought in the Vietnam War. He still had a bullet scar on his knee. I was fascinated by his experience. I didn't mind *aiming*, because as we did the exercise we could still talk freely.

My hand grenade throwing was terrible. I could not reach the required distance, which was 20 meters, no matter how hard I practised. I didn't know why, as I had all this energy and strong arms - that was why I was good at Bars when I was a gymnast, but somehow, I just could not throw far. My technique was incorrect, some boys told me. One boy even showed me how he arched his back and then swung his arm. Oh boy, he threw the grenade at least 50 meters. He said watching me throwing the grenade was like watching me dancing in a ballet. The soldier who was in charge of our class said I would have killed myself first if I had to throw that grenade at our enemies. I tried very hard, but in the end, I still failed the test.

The most exciting thing about the military training was the shooting test at the end using real guns. We were each given nine bullets and a rifle. We had to load the gun and shoot three bullets each from three positions - laying down on our stomachs, squatting, and standing.

I was so nervous that I couldn't load the bullets. A classmate who used to be in the army helped me. Once I fired the bullet, the echo of the firing was so loud that my ears hurt. The force of the rebound of the rifle almost blew my shoulder away. I was so glad when it was over. My score altogether was 77 out of 90. Not bad, I thought.

We had a banquet when the military training ended. The canteen cooked many delicious dishes, and we were allowed to take the food to our dormitories. The girls went to the boys' rooms to eat together. Some boys got drunk, and we girls had to do the cleaning up afterwards. It wasn't much fun after all.

The three-week military training was great fun. I didn't want it to finish. But everything had to come to an end, I thought.

Lectures began again. The studies become more and more boring. I had to drag myself to the lectures and force myself to do the assignments. Those electrical circuits did not make any sense to me. I couldn't understand why you had to put a transistor here and there to get the radio to work. I was not interested in it at all. There were times when I was sitting in the classroom while trying to draw a tree outside the window, and I wished I was doing an arts degree. I have always liked the arts, paintings, music, architecture and so on.

I became quite close to one of the girls, Yun, whose bed was next to mine. We went to lectures together and we went to canteens together. While the other girls were all studying during the evenings (*every* evening, can you believe it!), we went out to dance parties, theatres, concerts and so on. In the latter years of university, there were dance parties every now and then, and there were theatre companies coming to our university to perform plays. Even if we stayed in the dormitory, we would listen to the radio.

Yun was a hard-working student during the first term of the first year, but after that term, for some reason, she changed - she couldn't sit still anymore. Later on, I found out that she was in love. She was going out with a man who was a few years older than we were and in the same class as us.

Yun didn't tell me this herself. At that time in our university, falling in love was forbidden. There was a special person in our department called 'student supervisor' who was especially in charge of our so-called 'student affairs'. If he found out that anyone was going out with someone, or a boy and a girl were seen walking together frequently, he would ask this person to come to his office and have a 'talk' with him or her. That talk would include the threat that when graduation comes, both parties involved would be deliberately sent to two different cities.

I guess Yun was scared that someone would know that she was going out with this boy and the news would be passed on to the department. Even though we were so close, there were those cold winter nights when we snuggled up in one of our single beds, she still kept her secret. But she told me one horrible thing that kept me thinking and feeling horrified every night when I went to bed for almost all my university life.

It was a physics lecture. It was one of those combined lessons when people from other departments would come and join us. We were in this huge classroom that had steps. Yun and I went to the back of the room on purpose because we knew it was going to be boring. We couldn't help chatting sometimes during a boring lecture. Sitting at the back, it would not be noticed if we talked.

In the middle of the lecture, Yun told me her story.

Yun's father died when she was 13 years old. He died of liver cancer, Yun said, and he was cremated in one of the government cremation centres in Xi'an, the city where the Terra Cotta Warriors were found. When the time came for the family to collect the ashes, her mother didn't go. She didn't know why her mother didn't want to go. So, she went to the cremation centre on her own to collect her father's ashes. She loved her father and brought the ashes home in an urn and hid them somewhere in the house.

For all those years she kept her father's ashes in the house. She didn't tell her mother as she was angry with her, she said. When she was admitted to the South China University of Technology in Guangzhou five years later, she brought her father's ashes with her in a suitcase.

'*Where is it now?*' I asked her after she finished.

'*It is in my suitcase,*' she said.

Her suitcase was on top of the empty bed just opposite mine. It was an old brown leather suitcase.

After that day in the physics lecture, every night when I went to bed I stared at the leather suitcase opposite me, thinking that Yun's father's ashes were there. *What was it like being burnt, becoming ashes, and stored in a jar? Where do people go after death? Would their spirit linger around their family members?* According to Chinese tradition, our ancestors are supposed to know what we are doing in this life. They would look after us if we give them enough paper money to spend in their world. Where is their world?

Life was just meaningless. This message still comes to me every now and then.

Although Yun and I were so close, I didn't tell her anything about how those years were to me when we returned to our parents after the Cultural Revolution, but I just told her lightly that I didn't get along well with my parents. That was all I could say. I didn't know how to express those mixed feelings inside me. Plus, I had this idea that she wouldn't be able to understand. In fact, in my mind, I kept thinking that nobody in the world would understand what my brother and I went through. I looked at my roommates and those boys in our class. They were so immature, so childish. *'What sort of experiences have they been through?'* I often wondered.

I kept all that was in my heart to myself. I constantly felt the loneliness; only my diary kept me company during those years. But I had this dream in me that grew stronger and stronger every day. I was going to find this man who would appear from nowhere and he would be on a white horse. He would be handsome, with long hair that flowed in the air when he rode the horse. He would come to my window and rescue me. My desk was just next to the window, so I often looked outside into the dark when I couldn't bear to read one more word of those boring technical books and dreamed away. He would be caring and sensitive, he would know exactly what I was thinking and know exactly what I meant if I was to put my hand out. He would be the one who would take all my pain away and look after me. We would live happily ever after, and all would be fine with my life; I wouldn't feel this loneliness and emptiness inside anymore. I would laugh and smile a lot. We would have children, of course, and I would never, never, ever leave my children to anyone. I swear! I would love them with all my heart no matter what happened.

With this ideal man in my mind, all the boys around me seemed so dull. All they knew was studying and studying, nothing else. I kept my chin up, and wouldn't let anyone near me while I was waiting for this dream man to appear.

The power to all the dormitories would go off at 10:00 pm every night at our university. This was to prevent some manic students from studying through the night and destroying their health, I suppose. We had to have everything ready and be in bed before the lights went out, otherwise, we would be totally in the dark.

It was quite a funny scene sometimes, watching the girls in the building, running around in the corridor or shower rooms, yelling at each other to hurry up. There were only ten showers in the whole building which accommodated about 400 girls. And there was no hot water. In summer, the queue was unbearable, while in winter the cold water made my hair stand up. I never liked having a cold shower, even in the boiling hot summer.

I was glad when the power went off. It meant no more books, and no assignments. Every night when I went to bed, I remember, I had this transistor radio beside my pillow which I'd turn on and listen to music. The music soothed my heart.

China started to open its door to the rest of the world in the 1980s. Western music started to be broadcast on radios. I remember when I first heard the cello music 'Death of a Swan'. I was so touched that I could visualize the swan's elegant dance and fight before she dies.

First, I started to listen to short pieces of western classical music, mainly violin and piano work. Then I moved on to more complicated ones, such as symphonies, piano and violin concertos from Beethoven, Chopin, Tchaikovsky, Bach, Handel, and more.

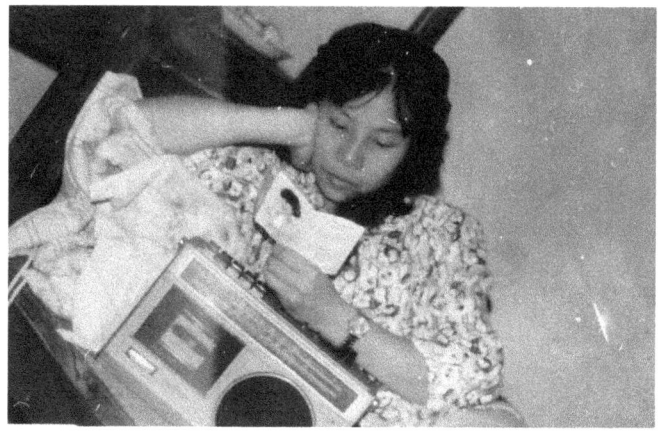

Me and my stereo on my bed, 1980 at South China University of Technology.

'*Why?*' I often asked myself, '*does this foreign music from one or two hundred years ago, and from countries that were so far away from China, seem to understand me?*' They expressed the sad, lonely, joyful, and all sorts of feelings, that I wasn't able to express. I felt as if there was a soft hand gently stroking my heart every time I listened to this music; the heart that had a hole in it and would never stop bleeding.

I sank myself into this ocean of the music world. Often the music would play itself in my head. I sometimes felt joy, but more often, sadness. I was on this lonely journey of life where I was all by myself, and there was music in the background that kept me company. There seemed to be a special link between me and the music that I listened to, and only the music and I could understand each other.

At that time, not many people in China understood western classical music. I had no one to talk to, and this kept me even more at a distance from the rest of the class.

Sometimes I talked to Yun a little. We went to concerts together a number of times - but she had not developed an enthusiasm towards classical music. She would go to concerts with me, but she showed no emotions. Maybe she was like me, unable to express any feelings; she had been through a lot in her 18 years of life, having to keep her father's ashes in a secret place in her home when she was only 13.

Yun had a schoolmate whom I shall call Gigi. Gigi and Yun went to the same high school in Xi'an. While Yun came to Guangzhou for her university study, Gigi went to Shanghai. He was admitted to the Department of Architecture at one of the leading universities in Shanghai, Tongji University.

Yun and Gigi kept writing to each other. Every time when Yun received his letter, I would always know that it was from Gigi because he always used the same plain, big white envelope. He always used a black ink pen and had beautiful handwriting. He always wrote 'Miss' on the envelope. No one used Miss, Mr, or Mrs on envelopes in China, we all used *Comrade*. 'He is so special!' I thought to myself.

G talked a lot about art and music in his letters to Yun. Music and Arts Appreciation was one of his subjects in achieving his degree. Yun sometimes gave his letters to me to read because she knew I was interested in music and arts.

He would write long letters and talk about how he felt when he listened to this and that music. All the European architecture, old or new, that he described in his letter really fascinated me. I felt he was so knowledgeable about the arts.

I became one of his secret admirers. 'He must be my dream man!' Many times I thought about this.

Gigi became my husband many years later.

In the second year of university, one of the PE teachers at the university wanted to organize a gymnastics team. My department recommended me to her. The teacher who recruited me to this department had read my file history. Everyone in China had a 'Party File' kept by the authorities. This file would record anything that may interest the Party, as well as what you did in the past. She knew that I was a gymnast before; in fact, she recruited me because of my gymnastics background, although my academic score was not as high, just four points above the university entry line.

I had never thought that I would pick up gymnastics again after I left Wenzhou. Those feelings of pride, the hard work and the joy of achievement had become a treasured memory and I had buried them in the bottom of my heart. Now I was fat and old (18 years was too old for gymnastics!). I couldn't possibly do gymnastics again.

But I joined the team, and for the following three years I won the first All Around, and three of the four Apparatus at the University Gymnastic Tournament of Guangzhou District for three consecutive years. After those years of training, I was sure I'd be better than most gymnasts because they were, in my opinion, amateurs.

We trained in the late afternoons two times a week after lectures. Most of the time I was helping other teammates improve their skills. I didn't have to do much because the routines were quite simple. I felt really good helping others achieve their best, and they liked my coaching, too.

By the time we finished the training, the canteen was usually closed. Our 'big sister' Zhixin would get dinner for me earlier. She did that for almost three years without complaining at all. I was very grateful to her.

Once again, gymnastics became one of the most enjoyable pastimes in my life. It released my frustration from the boring study and exams that I had to put up with. It also helped me forget the pain and unhappiness that I had brought from home.

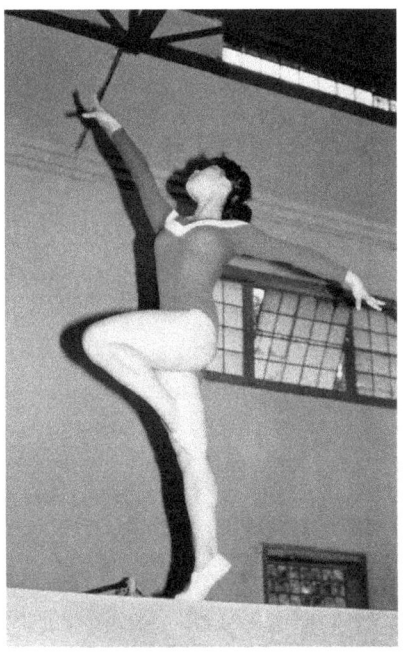

Gymnastic training at SCUT University

Feng's Big Exam Time

In 1980, it was Feng's turn to participate in the national exams for entering university. He didn't do very well at school and my parents were not pleased with his results. I was getting very worried about what would happen if he didn't pass the exam. Dad probably would kill him, or Feng would kill himself, I imagined. At the time, we had moved into a two-room place. My parents had one room. The other room was divided into two small rooms; one was Feng's bedroom and the other was our living and dining area, with no door between the two sections.

Feng had to spend every moment of spare time there to study, with Father's eyes on his back almost every night. If he didn't study, Father would be very unhappy. Besides, there was nowhere to go anyway. He had no close friends to go to, having left all his friends behind in Wenzhou. Two years before, when I was preparing for the big exam, when I had my own bedroom upstairs where nobody knew what I was doing once I shut the door - I had my freedom then. Feng didn't.

Feng was deeply depressed and stopped talking to anyone. Like me, he showed interest in history and arts, but neither he nor my parents recognized it. Following my parents' will, he also went to the exams for an engineering degree.

And he failed.

I was not surprised. The question was, after we knew the result, how was he going to live this whole year staying at home doing nothing and waiting for next year's exam? I still remembered the first six months when we first arrived in Guangzhou, when I didn't go to school until September. The days were extremely long, and they were almost unbearable. I didn't think that Feng would survive this period because his relationship with our parents was worse than mine at the time. I didn't want him to go through what I did.

I went and visited a teacher from my middle school who used to teach us Chinese. I knew she was very influential at No. 2 Middle School. At the time, No. 2 Middle School offered a few catch-up classes for those students who failed the exams and would be going for the following year. Places were very tight as 99.9% of high school graduates would fail the exam. I asked my teacher to please use her influence to get Feng a place in these classes and she did. Feng went into my school - one of the top middle schools in Guangzhou. Although he wasn't willing, I persuaded him to go. I told him that it would be miserable for him to stay at home and look at our parents' disapproving faces; he'd be better off going to school. Thank God he listened and gave himself up to the course.

Feng wasn't keen on studying, but the school gave students a lot of exercises and homework to do, from which Feng benefited. The teachers at the school pushed as far as they could, because the percentage of the students who would enter universities would directly affect the school's reputation and name.

I spent the week at university, only going home on Saturdays to stay the night at home. I would return to university on Sunday night. I was not sure how Feng got along with my parents. I don't think it was pleasant. There was simply no communication between him and our parents. They didn't ask how we were, and we certainly didn't tell them how we felt. At the time, both Feng and I resented our parents immensely and wished so much that we could return to our grandma.

When Father was not happy, he would not say anything to us. He wouldn't say what it was that we did wrong; maybe it was simply he was stressed from work. Sometimes we heard a bang on the door or a sound from somewhere that he had made deliberately. We knew he was angry. One time, it was midnight, and we heard a sound that sounded like a mug being thrown on the terra-cotta floor. I guessed that it must have been something Feng did during the day that Father was not happy about. It couldn't have been me because I had just got back from uni. Feng got up and walked out the door and didn't come back that night. Later we found out that he went to a neighbour's place - they had a son who became friends with Feng.

We asked him to come back the second day.

Again, nothing was said or discussed.

The condition we lived in was not pleasant. Although we had two rooms, there was no kitchen, no bathroom, and no toilet. 10 metres away on the other side of the building, there were five or six stoves belonging to the families living on our floor where we cooked our meals. Washing was in another place. We had to use buckets to carry water from the shared tap. Life was difficult and we hardly saw any happy, smiley faces around.

Every time when Father returned home from work, the first thing I did was to take a peek at his face. Was he happy today or was he upset again? Feng and Father could never stay in the same room. Feng tried to avoid him all the time. Sometimes the silence was so intense that you could hear a pin drop. Most of the time we believed that it was something either Feng or I did that made him unhappy. But thinking back now, he would not be happy no matter what we did - how can one be happy after what he experienced through the Cultural Revolution? I was lucky that I lived at the university dormitory for four years. Whatever happened at home, I was able to break away from it for a number of days. But the shadow was with me all the time. My diary was full of sadness and despair. *'An unhappy family is the saddest tragedy that a person can experience'*, I wrote in my diary. How I wished and craved for a warm peaceful family.

Grandma came to visit us in 1981. She also wanted Feng to go to university. At the time, getting into university was the only way for us younger generation to have a secure job in the future. The government stopped sending high school graduates to the remote countryside after 1977. However, there were no jobs waiting for us after we finished high school. Every year there were tens of thousands of high school graduates finishing schooling who couldn't find a job. These people were what we called *'Job-waiting Youths'* at the time.

Grandma hoped that her love and help with the housework would ease some tension that had built up between our parents and us, particularly between Father and Feng. She knew that we didn't get along with our parents. A couple of times she said to us that our parents didn't know how to bring up children because they never had to. She was angry at Father sometimes; she said he was too strict towards us.

The days of the exams were fast approaching. Tuesday the 7th of July, 1981 was the first day of exams which would take three days.

Two days before the exam, Feng became sick. His tonsils swelled up; he was coughing and had a temperature of 39°C. Mum took him to the hospital and the doctor gave him an injection. On Monday, his condition was worse. Not only did his temperature not drop, but he also started vomiting. He vomited blood! The doctor said it was caused by the medicine.

I was worried to death. Mum went away on business again. Dad was unhappy again. He said Feng was weak! Why did he have to be sick at this time? He showed no other feeling but frustration.

'Did he have control over when he was going to be sick?' I said to myself. Grandma had a fight with Dad because she thought that he was being ridiculous. He didn't care about us at all. The only thing he could do was get angry.

When I came home from university that weekend, I had a look at everyone's faces. I knew exactly what was going on and swallowed tears as I tried to cheer everyone up. It was an important time in Feng's life. Probably in everybody's life in the family! Who knows what would happen if he failed the exam again?

'Why do people have to live?' I wrote in my diary. I had lived 20 years of my life, during which half of the time I was happy and half not. *'Why is there so much unhappiness in the world? What does my future look like?'* I couldn't see.

Feng went to the exams. In the middle of the exam, he had to ask for permission to go out because he was so sick, but he finished the exams.

Then it was the waiting-for-results time. Everyone was quiet. The atmosphere felt like we were waiting for a final sentence on whether or not we were going to live. All we could hear was the heavy sighs from deep inside our parent's bodies.

Grandma left for Dalian where Aunt Meijun and her family

lived soon after Feng's exam. All of Grandma's life was devoted to helping her two daughters and five grandchildren who lived in three different places. Miao was still struggling with his dancing and acting career in Wenzhou.

There was a half-smoked cigarette left in the ashtray on the day Grandma left. *When will I see her again?* I wrote in my diary.

Feng passed the exams. His result was 273.5 and the entry score was 234 for colleges. His result was not good enough to enter universities, but he could go to a college. Who cared? He had somewhere to go now, away from home, which was such an unhappy place for him to be. *Thank you. Thank you, whoever is out there*, I said to myself. *This family is going to have some peaceful times now, hopefully.*

When it was time to choose a school and a major, Feng insisted on going to the Sailor's College. He chose to study to become a radio operator on a ship. I knew exactly what was on his mind when he chose the college and the department. He wanted to stay away from home when he finished his studies. The only place he could go was to work on a ship that would be drifting on the high sea most of the year. He didn't have to stay with my parents again. I felt very sad. But there was nothing I could do.

Feng moved into Guangzhou Sailor's College. Colleges are like universities. They are also self-contained little kingdoms. Like me, Feng stayed at the college during the week and came home on the weekends. Life was good in our family for a while. On my 20th birthday, Mum and Dad prepared a small banquet to celebrate, firstly, Feng's admission to college, then my 20th birthday. I was so very happy.

Graduation

After my 20th birthday, my fourth year at university started. I still couldn't concentrate on studying. My mind was elsewhere, or perhaps nowhere. I couldn't see my future. I didn't know what to do. I went to movies and concerts a lot.

While I tried to occupy myself with entertainment, my body was not functioning perfectly well. My right arm felt numb, and my right hand shook sometimes when I was writing. I discovered a lump on my right breast - just under my arm. The lump was as big as an olive and was not very hard. It didn't worry me much. When I was a girl in Wenzhou, I remember I used to wish that I would be sick so I could get some attention. Once when I was really sick, I was off school for two weeks and couldn't go to the gym. Coach Xia came to visit me and gave me a tin of biscuits. I remember that afternoon. It was late afternoon. The Sun sprinkled golden rays through the tree leaves. I had almost recovered from the illness and was lying in a bamboo armchair in the courtyard, feeling the warmth of the sun shining on me and holding the tin of biscuits in my hand. I was really happy. I often imagined myself lying in a hospital bed, covered with white linen, with friends coming to visit me. This scene made me happy, so I was not afraid of being sick at all. On the contrary, somehow, I felt that it was probably my wish come true.

I didn't tell mother. I didn't tell anyone except one girl called Jie who lived in the opposite room in our dormitory. She needed to see a doctor for her tooth at that time.

In our university, there was a medical clinic. The clinic treated common sicknesses such as colds, sore throats etc. For diseases that were more serious, the doctors in the clinic would refer us to hospitals outside our uni.

I was told to go to the hospital to have a check-up. Jie had something else that needed attention, so we took a bus to the Third Hospital of Guangzhou. I didn't know which department I should go to. I thought the lump was inside my body so it must be the internal disease department. I paid for a registration ticket for the Internal Disease Department.

I was too shy to tell the doctor the truth. I just said I had a lump under my arm. He couldn't find it. Then I pointed out the place and he said: *'You have a lump in your breast, and you need to see a surgeon.'*

This meant that I had to queue up at the central office window again and buy another registration ticket for the surgery department. I hesitated. I almost wanted to give up.

The doctor looked at me and thought for a while. He asked me to wait and went out.

He came back with another doctor. He said the other doctor was a surgeon. The surgeon looked at the lump and moved it around. *'It's probably just a soft tissue cyst, it shouldn't be serious,'* he said, and then left.

The Internal Department doctor prescribed eight penicillin injections to take back to my university clinic. *'Oh no, not the penicillin injections again,'* I thought to myself. I still remember the injection I had when I was in Hangzhou for the national gymnastics competition. It was so painful. But I took them back to the nurses in our own clinic anyway.

I had four injections before the nurse asked me, out of her curiosity, what it was that I needed to have so many penicillin injections for. I looked perfectly healthy and energetic in her eyes. I told her that I had a lump on my breast.

'You need to see a herbalist', she said. *'Stop the injections. Penicillin is for people who have serious infections. Go and see a herbalist; they help,'* she said matter-of-factly.

So I stopped the injections and went to another hospital. This time I went to the Chinese herbal department. I had to queue up again. The doctor who had the least patients was a young girl. She must have been a new graduate, I thought. I didn't want to wait for too long, so I joined her queue.

I watched her consulting patients in front of me. There were so many patients waiting that she had no time to talk to them in detail at all. She didn't even touch the patient's hands (It is a required procedure for a herbalist to feel the patient's pulse). She just kept writing the formulas, according to what the patients told her.

When it was my turn, I told her what the surgeon said about the soft tissue cyst. *'Oh,'* she said, and took out a book. She copied a formula from the book. *'Try this for a week; see how you go, come back if you need to.'* She didn't even take a look at me, I thought, as I was too shy to take off my clothes in front of so many other patients and doctors.

I had to tell Mother because I needed to boil the herbs. She took it quietly. I drank all the herbal tea. It was such a bitter yellow liquid. The lump seemed smaller and softer, and my hand stopped shaking so I didn't bother to have more herbs. I left it like that, and the lump disappeared over the years.

According to Chinese medicine theory, a cyst or lump in the body indicates that the person has repressed feelings or stress, and if you repress your feelings for long enough, they would either generate some growth somewhere in your body or you become sick in another form. I always wondered if my lump was related to the change in my life from Grandma's Wenzhou to my parents' Guangzhou. What a change. I wish I hadn't lived those two years.

For the fourth year of university, lectures were reduced. Instead, we had to do a graduate project and write a thesis. Some people chose to design a TV, some chose to design a CPU board (central processing unit; all computers need it to operate) that had some control functions. I chose to design a transistor radio. I thought it was the easiest and most visible thing one could design. I had one next to my pillow! I listened to it every night.

There were many books on radio design. You just had to copy part of this, part of that and combine them together to become yours. I passed my graduate design with a B.

Looking back, English was my best subject. Wei sent me a set of four English textbooks called 'The Basics'. They were stories and real situation-based English textbooks published in England. The stories were very funny. Wei said she ordered them from her factory for me.

At that time, learning English was very popular. China had just started to open its doors to the West. English books were everywhere.

Although we only learnt English for the first year of university, I kept reading those English books that Wei sent to me. I also liked to read English novels at the time. I read the English version of Jane Eyre and it became one of my favourite western novels. I liked the character so much that I even changed my name to Jane after I came to Australia. I still remember the first sentence that reads: *'It was impossible to take a walk that afternoon...'*

The time had come for graduation. The presentation of our final project was stressful, but everyone passed. I obtained my bachelor's degree in Engineering in Radio Technology in 1982.

I felt sad that it was time to leave university. I always liked dormitory life - sharing with other friends. I made a few good friends, most of whom were from other provinces.

It was a very important time in our lives when it came to the assignment of a workplace. The department decided what we would do and where we would go - we had no choice at all.

I was assigned to the Guangdong Bureau of Standards. I didn't know what it was at the time. My parents wanted me to stay in Guangzhou. The Bureau sounded all right to my parents, so we didn't argue about it. We didn't have a choice anyway.

Yun was sent to the army in Hunang province. She was warned in the first year when she was going out with a boy that if she kept seeing her boyfriend they would be separated on graduation - and indeed they were, even though her boyfriend's father was in a high position. They couldn't get permission for her to stay in Guangzhou. Her boyfriend stayed. Later, it took him two years to get Yun back to Guangzhou, then they got married.

I was very sad to see everybody go. Some went back to where they came from; some to other provinces; all were sent to the positions that the university authorities assigned to them.

That was the end of my university life. Although I didn't like the study that much, I enjoyed being away from home, away from my parents. I had some freedom, to a certain degree.

Gerhard

The first day I went to Guangdong Bureau of Standards, the personnel officer to whom I was to report wasn't there. I was told to come back another day. The company that I was to work in had four stories; every floor consisted of offices that sat 4-10 people. The Bureau was the highest authority in charge of all the provincial standards or regulations for every product. That is to say, if manufacturers or industries wanted to establish a new standard for a product, they had to get the approval of Guangdong Bureau of Standards. The Bureau had a number of departments. They were, from my memory, Accounting, Human Resources, and Standards Department. There was also a library that had a large collection of provincial, national, and international standards. We called this library *Guangdong Standard Information Institute*.

I was assigned to this Institute. I didn't think it had anything to do with the subjects I studied at university, but there was nothing I could do to change it. The government told us what to do.

There were over 40 people working in this Bureau. Eight people worked in the library; I was one of them. When people come to look for certain standards, we received them, making photocopies when they were required. Most of the time there was nothing much to do. Most people came to work with a cup of tea and read newspapers all day.

People who worked in the library were mostly young. We chatted all day.

We started working at 8:00 am in the morning and finished at 12:00. Then we'd have our lunch at the company canteen. Those people who lived nearby would go home to have their lunch at home. Then we would have a one and half-hour nap in the office; people would lie on top of their desks to have a sleep.

The afternoon session started at 2:00 pm and finished at 5:30 pm. At the time, I wasn't brave enough to ride a bicycle to work. The distance between home and work was approximately 10 kilometres. My workplace was on the south side of the Pearl River. My home was far north of the river. Every day, I would take the bus for 30 minutes, then walk for another 20 minutes to work. I didn't mind the walk, but waiting for the overcrowded bus really frustrated me.

The bus was always crowded during rush hour in Guangzhou. Sometimes two or three buses passed by where I couldn't get on because there was simply no room -unless you had enough strength to pull someone off the bus and throw yourself in! I always hated to have to get the bus, especially in the summertime. Summer in Guangzhou is very hot and humid. The bus was so full, with people standing one against the other. There were bodies on your front, sides and back. The smell of body odour was terrible. On many occasions, I could feel a man's penis pressed against my back or side, and with an erection! I felt sick. It filled me with dread just to think about getting on the bus every morning and afternoon.

I worked for the Bureau for about two years. I didn't use the knowledge I gained from university at all; most of the time I felt very bored.

And then Guangdong Bureau of Metrology was merged with Guangdong Standard Bureau. Under the Guangdong Bureau of Metrology, there was a testing laboratory where clients brought their equipment to be tested and adjusted according to provincial standards. I took the opportunity and applied for a transfer as I wanted some hands-on experience in the field that I had studied for four years. Although I was not overly interested in radio engineering when I enrolled in university, I thought it was my duty to be able to use what I had learnt. After all, I was given the four years of study free of charge. It was time for me to give something back.

My application was granted. Changing jobs within the same company was relatively easier than moving between two different companies. I was sent to work in the laboratory, testing digital voltage meters - so I was quite happy.

The laboratory was a very clean place. The whole centre was air-conditioned. To go into the laboratory, people had to take their shoes off and wear white lab coats, and it was very quiet inside. I really liked the environment and worked there for nearly a year.

One afternoon, I was working in the laboratory by myself. It was very quiet, so I switched on the radio. I was listening to classical music on the radio when I heard a voice saying 'Hello' behind me. I got such a shock. I turned around and saw a tall, bearded foreigner standing there. Next to him was our laboratory leader. Because they took their shoes off, I did not even hear them coming in.

At the time, my English was very limited, and I wasn't prepared for such a visit. I couldn't say anything, just stood there. A translator explained what this room was for. He didn't introduce me to the foreigner. It's typical. A person like me who is young and has no title is not important in the leader's mind; not worth introducing. The bearded Westerner looked at me. I could feel he was quite interested in knowing what my role was at the laboratory. But he didn't say anything. Perhaps he thought I didn't understand English at all.

And then they left, as quietly as they came.

Later I was told that this foreigner was from West Germany. He came from a world-renowned testing institute called VDE. He was here to talk to the Bureau to see if there was any possibility of establishing a relationship between the two laboratories.

A year later I met this German engineer again. I learnt that his name was Gerhard. He was the deputy director of VDE Testing and Certification Institute in West Germany. He paid his second visit to our Bureau because our laboratory wanted to become VDE's representative in Asia. This time I was in a different laboratory.

Gerhard visited our laboratory - 1985.

In order to become VDE's representative in Asia, our Bureau decided that it was necessary to set up a brand-new laboratory with the most advanced equipment. The top floor of the main building was reserved for this laboratory which was to be called the Quality Supervision and Testing Centre of Guangdong, as well as VDE Asian Testing Centre (this name was dropped later because VDE didn't think we qualified with their standard). The director of our Bureau approached me. He knew I had studied radio engineering and my English was quite good compared to other colleagues at the Bureau. He asked me whether or not I would like to be transferred to the new laboratory, which might have the opportunity for me to go to Germany. I was delighted to take up this golden opportunity.

I was put in the group that was going to set up testing sites and determine the equipment needed for Radio Interference Testing of electronic products. I was very enthusiastic as, finally, I was going to use the knowledge that I learnt from four years of university study.

Gerhard came to inspect our site and to discuss the equipment we were going to purchase from Germany through VDE.

At the time, our Centre had about 20 staff. Almost half of them were administrative staff who, most of the time, had nothing to do during work hours. The rest were engineers or technicians. Among the technical staff, there were two people who knew some English. One was Zhu, the official translator whom the company recruited from outside because of his English background. The other was me. Zhu translated in official situations like meetings, dinners, and the like. I interpreted in informal situations, such as showing Gerhard around our Centre, discussing our plans, equipment, etc. We got along well. I felt, to a certain extent, Gerhard and I shared a lot of similar views. One time he pointed to the administrative staff who sat there, and whose eyes were following us whenever we went...

'Who are these people? What do they do in this Centre?' he asked me.

'They are our administrative staff, like political officers, HR, bookkeepers, cleaners.' There were a few people whose positions I couldn't explain because I didn't really know what they were there for, myself. When we walked past our Political Office, he asked me again what the three people who were sitting inside did. I said these people made sure that our work was on the right track according to communist rules and that we 'behaved' correctly.

We both smiled at each other, knowing that such an office was just a waste of money, people, and space. Every workplace in China would have a Political Unit then. People working in this office were in charge of each staff member's personal files - what they did in past political movements, what their views were, what their family background was, etc. These political files were going to follow us all our lives wherever we went. They were sent from our current workplace to the next by special mail. We ourselves never knew what was inside those files.

One afternoon I was chatting with Gerhard. I said that he didn't look like a German.

'Why?' he said. 'Is it because I have brown eyes?' he joked.

'Germans to me are very serious people,' I said. 'They often have this serious look on their face. But you joke a lot,' I said.

I commented on this only because I acted as a translator for three German engineers who visited our Bureau before, and they were serious people who didn't laugh much during their visit to China.

Gerhard replied: *'I am a serious person, but I also like laughs and joking around.'*

I found our conversation very pleasant. He was a very easygoing person. I liked chatting with him whenever we had a moment. I found out then he was married with two sons; they were eight and six.

One day, I said to him, casually, that since this Centre provided an opportunity for technical staff to visit Germany, I'd like to learn some German just in case I was chosen to go. A few days later when another engineer from VDE arrived from Germany to join him, Gerhard gave me a little English-German dictionary.

'You may need this one day when you learn German,' he said.

I was caught by surprise. I was embarrassed as I received the book in front of all our leaders and colleagues. *'How could he be so thoughtful and have acted so quickly?'* I thought. What would our leaders think of me, since none of them received any gifts?

It turned out that he sent a fax to ask his colleague who was coming to China to bring him this dictionary.

One day Gerhard said to me: *'Why do I have to go to a restaurant for lunch every day? I want to have lunch at your canteen like everyone else. It's a waste of time and money.'*

I told him that our leader considered that the food in our canteen was not good enough. The restaurants would be better.

'But everyone else eats there,' he said. 'So can I.'

Every day, our company driver took Gerhard in our company car to a restaurant for lunch, accompanied by a couple of leaders. I think they liked to eat at the restaurants themselves.

'I'd like to be like everyone else,' he insisted.

But our leaders stressed that he was our guest. He should be treated specially.

After 10 days of inspection and discussion, Gerhard's visit came to an end. He was leaving Guangzhou by Guangzhou-Hong Kong train on Friday. But he said to our leader suddenly:

'I've decided to postpone my train to Hong Kong for one day. I'm leaving on Saturday.'

He said, 'I'd like to spend one more day in Guangzhou to look around.' He added, 'Could I have your permission to have Miss Xing as my interpreter please?'

I told my leader about Gerhard's request. Mr Liu, our political leader, glanced at me from the corner of his eyes. He said:

'Of course, we would be very pleased to arrange some sightseeing for you. Our driver will take you.'

'Thank you very much for your considerate thought,' Gerhard replied: 'but no. I'd like to have some time on my own. If it is not too much trouble, I'd like to have Miss Xing as my interpreter and guide please.'

Gerhard didn't like to be driven in our company car at all. He didn't like our driver. 'That driver is going to prison one day,' he said to me. 'He used the wrong gear at the wrong speed, was *speeding all the time and tried to overtake while we were on the bridge and couldn't see the oncoming traffic,'* he explained.

Knowing that Gerhard drove a car himself in Germany, I thought maybe he had his grounds. Traffic in China was chaotic. There were no rules. People don't follow the lights.

His life was in a stranger's hands in a foreign country, I thought. For me, I had no idea how car gears worked (what was a gear?), nor did I have any knowledge of what the correct traffic rules were. I had never been to any other country besides China.

He even suggested jokingly that he and I swap. *'You go with the car to be taken to and from work; I'll use your bicycle,'* he said. I loved his humour.

'That would be good,' I said, imagining myself sitting inside the black sedan and looking through the window. I wouldn't have to struggle on the bike through the crowd every day, no matter what was happening outside, even if the rain was like a knife, or the weather hot like a stove, I would be safe. I thought Gerhard would have liked the experience, too, riding a bicycle among thousands of people - or as we describe the scene - the sea of people, being stared or pointed at. People in China hadn't seen many big-nose Westerners then. When they saw one, they couldn't help staring at him.

Swapping our roles was, of course, out of question. But Gerhard's dream of riding a bicycle like an ordinary Chinese person did come true.

Liu agreed to Gerhard's request, even though he wasn't very happy. Saying no to a foreigner would not be considered polite in our customs. Saying no to someone like Gerhard whose relationship with us decided our Centre's future was even worse. Liu didn't want to upset our precious guest.

Gerhard thanked Liu for allowing me to have a day off work to accompany him.

The following day, I had the most pleasant and interesting day of my life.

Gerhard made the arrangement that we were to have breakfast together at the White Swan Hotel where he was staying. He was going to meet me at the reception. At first, I hesitated. I didn't know what our leaders were going to say when they found out. Would I be punished later? But the experience was more attractive. Having breakfast in one of the top 5-star hotels in Guangzhou was a novelty to me. I had not had such an experience before, so I agreed.

I arrived at the hotel at 8:15 am that morning. Gerhard was already waiting for me at the lift. We went upstairs and I found myself entering a big restaurant with lots of gold-coloured decorations. The restaurant was so quiet and almost empty. What a difference between here and the outside world, I thought.

The White Swan Hotel was situated on a small island right next to the Pearl River. It had 33 stories. The outside wall of the whole building was covered with white tiles. *'Like a white swan floating on the river.'* That's how its name was chosen. It was a project invested in by a well-known Hong Kong businessman.

From the restaurant, we could see the Pearl River clearly. We chatted as we had our breakfast. Outside the window, on the river, there was a middle-aged woman rowing a boat against the current. It was a very windy day. The woman was carrying a baby on her back. Gerhard and I both watched this woman and her boat. We didn't know where she was heading. It seemed to us that she rowed for a long time and didn't achieve much distance. She was still in our sight. She couldn't go very fast no matter how hard she rowed.

'Women in China have to work very hard,' Gerhard commented. I nodded my head. Life was very much a struggle. Just like that woman in the boat, I thought to myself.

After breakfast, Gerhard suggested we go for a bike ride. There was a little shop next to the White Swan Hotel that had bicycles for hire. Gerhard had already spotted this shop when he was taken in and out of work before. The shop was mainly for foreigners who stayed at the Swan Hotel and wanted to have the experience of riding a bicycle in Guangzhou. The locals would have had at least one or two bicycles in their families. They wouldn't need to rent a bicycle.

Gerhard got his bike without any problem - a very old 28-inch man's bicycle. He took out a local map. 'He is such a well-organized person,' I thought to myself.

'We'll go this way, to this road and through this park.' He showed me the map. *'What do you think?'* he asked.

I hesitated. The way he showed me was a quite long ride, and it was the main road with a lot of traffic. I was not sure what sort of bicycle skills Gerhard had. So I showed him a different way which was quieter and safer.

'We can have lunch at my parents' place,' I said. My parents' flat was not far from the park.

'That's great,' he said.

We set off down the road. We zigzagged through half of Guangzhou's back roads and went through Yue-Xiu Park where the well-known Five Goats statue was. Then we arrived at the building where my parents' flat was. Our building caretaker looked at Gerhard and me with curiosity, but she didn't say anything. She let us in because she knew me.

I showed Gerhard our flat. It was a three-bedroom flat on the 7th floor. I wasn't prepared for such a visit. The flat was full of dust. I showed him my parents' bedroom, my room, and a spare room for my brother when he came back from the sea.

'Oh, you have a spare room,' he said. *'So next time I come to China I could stay at your place?'* he joked again.

'My parents would kill me,' I said. Inviting a stranger, especially a big-nosed foreigner to stay in our house would certainly scare my parents to death.

I pointed at a box in my room and said:

'That's my guitar.'

'Do you play guitar?' he asked, very surprised.

'A little,' I replied.

I'd always wanted to be able to play a musical instrument, but I didn't have any chance in my childhood, as we couldn't afford one. When I entered the university, I used the first month's scholarship money and bought myself a guitar. I self-taught, following a magazine and learnt to play a few pieces.

'Can you play?' I asked Gerhard.

'I can't really play, but I can sing with it.' he answered. *'Can you play me a piece?'*

I played a short piece called Long, Long Ago. It was a piece of western music. He knew the tune and hummed along as I played.

'It's your turn,' I gave the guitar to him.

'What do you want to hear?' he asked me.

'Anything,' I said. *'Do you know how to sing Leaving on a Jet Plane?'* I liked this song, I told him.

'Ah, 'Leaving on a Jet Plane' by John Denver,' he said, *'but I don't remember the words.'*

'I have the words.' I jumped up and took out a list of English song words that I had carefully typed. These were my favourite English songs.

He read out the titles as he flipped through the pages: *'Leaving on a Jet Plane, Streets of London, Vincent, Where Have All the Flowers Gone, Blowing in the Wind, Both Sides Now … Wow, you even have Both Sides Now. I know all these songs,'* he said. *'How amazing… I know now how you learnt your English.'*

'Yes,' I said. *'I have two tapes of my favourite English songs. I listen to them over and over, write down the words and then type them up.'*

We both sang through all those songs. He played the guitar while we were singing. When we came to the folk song, Both Sides Now, he told me where he learnt this song. He said when he was on a business trip to Dublin, he met a local girl. She invited him to her family and taught him this song on the night while they were by the fire.

'I've looked at life, from both sides now, from up and down, and still, somehow, I really don't know life at all...' we sang together, both excited with the discovery that we shared similar interests.

The song described how I felt at that moment, really. Here I was. I'd been longing for a soul mate for all my life, and there he was, a foreigner from such a faraway country, who seemed to share similar views on the meaning of life with me - through the songs we sang. *'I really don't know life at all...'*

Gerhard was tall, fit, and handsome. He had such a free spirit; witty and humorous. I liked him a lot. We got along so well.

Gerhard continued singing while I cooked fried rice for us. We washed our fried rice down with Coke - the only drink I could find in our fridge.

After lunch, it was nearly two o'clock. We started to head back to the Hotel as Gerhard had invited Zhu to the hotel and they were going to play tennis. He invited me to play with them.

We got back and rented tennis rackets from the hotel.

It was my first time playing tennis. I didn't know how to play at all. Although I had a gymnastics background, that had nothing to do with tennis. I could hardly hit a single ball! I had to run around picking up the balls. Both Gerhard and I were relieved when Zhu arrived. Perhaps Gerhard found it more embarrassing for putting me into this awkward position than me. But I enjoyed the whole experience. It was great fun.

On the second day, Gerhard was leaving Guangzhou for Hong Kong. I went to the train station to say farewell to him. Mr Zhu and another leader were already there. The guard stopped us before we entered the platform. He said only one person was allowed in. Our leader wanted to go in, but he needed Zhu as an interpreter. So, Gerhard asked me to go in and said goodbye to Zhu and the leader.

When it was time for Gerhard to board the train, we shook hands goodbye. Gerhard pulled me closer and gave me a kiss on my cheek.

My fairytale-like experience with a foreigner ended. I felt so good when I was with him. I felt respected and more appreciated than I had ever felt from anyone else in my life. I was sad when he left.

I gave Gerhard a tape of those favourite folk songs of mine. I hoped that he would remember the time we spent together. I myself would treasure those fond memories forever.

Gigi

One November day in 1983, my university friend Yun rang me at work. She was in Guangzhou for a short visit to her boyfriend. The university sent her to Hunan when she finished her studies because of her romance with the boy in our class, which was against the university rules. I went to her boyfriend's place to see her. As we chatted, Yun gave me a letter to read. This letter was from her high school friend Gigi who was studying at Shanghai Tongji University - one of the top universities in China. In the letter, I remember, he described how he was moved by the music he listened to. It was Chopin's Piano Concerto No 2.

His letter touched my lonely heart. I had a similar feeling when I listened to classical music. That night when I got home, I wrote Gigi a letter. I knew he was studying at the Department of Architecture at Tongji University for his postgraduate degree. I was sure my letter would reach him without a problem.

My letter was short. In the letter I introduced myself and told him that I'd heard about him from Yun a long time ago when we started university - Yun often mentioned him. I said I knew he liked classical music and so did I. I said if he liked, we could exchange our thoughts about the music that we listened to in a letter.

Six days later, I had a reply. He said he would be delighted to write to me. He also sent me a black and white photo of himself, which I had already seen in Yun's photo album. He asked if he could have a photo of me so he would have some idea of whom he was writing to.

I sent him a photo of myself immediately. I deliberately chose one of my not-so-good photos because I believed that soul mates would not be put off by appearances.

We started to write to each other frequently, though I wrote more because I had the time. He was sometimes preoccupied with his studies. Again, waiting for the postman became the most important event in my life. I became restless if I hadn't received his letters which should have arrived by that day. Initially, we started to talk about music, but after a few letters we began to talk about everything; about the books we read, about our daily life, our families, our childhood, the past, and so on. In my heart, I already decided that he was my soul mate. I told myself that he would understand me. I told him a lot about myself, which I wouldn't have told to him if I were to talk to him face to face. He opened his heart too. He told me that he didn't have a very happy childhood either. His mother was very strict, and he was the eldest in the family. He cooked and did most of the housework when he was still in high school while his parents devoted their time to work. He had to look after his two younger sisters as well. He even learnt to sew clothes. He said he had too many responsibilities when he was little, and all these experiences made him an introverted person - quiet and thoughtful. That was exactly the sort of man I would have liked. I thought to myself - quiet and thoughtful.

It was close to Chinese New Year in 1984. The winter holiday was coming for university students. Gigi said he would like to come to Guangzhou to collect some information for his thesis, and also to meet me. I was so happy and nervous. What if he didn't like me when he saw me? What if we didn't get along well like we did when writing?

As the time drew closer, I was getting very excited and anxious. What was he like in real life? Although I had seen his photos, a real person would be different. With all these questions, as well as curiosity and excitement, I went to the train station to meet him.

As he walked towards me among all the other people who just got off the train, I recognised him immediately. He was very tall - I thought to myself, taller than I had imagined, and his skin was very white!

These were the two things I remembered when I first met Gigi.

We smiled at each other awkwardly, shook hands and slowly walked to the bus station.

'It's a fine day,' he said. *'It was cold and raining in Shanghai; we haven't seen the sun for a while.'*

'Why did he talk about the weather?' I thought to myself. After all the things we talked about in our letters? He could have talked about... I don't know, anything - about him, about me, about what we do, about our families. Why the weather?

I was so disappointed. In fact, I didn't know what to expect. I felt he was so distant. Nothing like the man I poured my heart out to, so I kept quiet. I didn't know what to say. We arrived at my parents' home. I had asked my parents to let Gigi stay in our spare room. Father nearly killed me when I asked him. He thought I was crazy to have a man I never met to stay in our home. But I insisted that he was a good student who was doing his master's research in Guangzhou and, obviously, a student wouldn't have money to stay in a hotel. I told Father that he is a good friend of Yun, whom my father knows well. Finally, he agreed.

For the following 10 days, Gigi went out to do his research during the day while I went to work as usual. In the evenings, we would go to a nearby park to have some time on our own. Sometimes I would take a day off work to accompany him to places, as he was not familiar with the streets in Guangzhou.

Our conversations didn't go well. We couldn't talk to each other as intimately as we did in our letters. *'What's going on,'* I thought, *'and why?'* Why was he so distant? I didn't know at the time that we both had our walls up and we didn't know how to break the barrier between us. I felt very disappointed. After 10 days, Gigi left for Shanghai. We shook hands again, as politely as when we first met.

The date was February 1984.

Gigi, Miao, Miao's girlfriend, and me in Guangzhou on my parent's balcony - 1985

But we continued writing. Things went back to normal again. I forgot all about the disappointing feelings I had when we talked face-to-face. I told him that I couldn't wait to see him again.

In May, an opportunity of visiting Shanghai arose from my work. Our leaders said that we should visit laboratories in other cities to see what they had done so we could learn from them. Shanghai was the biggest city in China. It was also an industrial centre. There are more companies and laboratories in Shanghai than in any other city in China. Therefore, there were more things to see, we convinced our leaders.

So, two colleagues and I planned to go to Shanghai to have a look at other laboratories and what they were doing. Because of the time limit, the leaders allowed us to travel by plane. It was my first time on an aeroplane. I was most excited about the whole trip.

I told Gigi that I was going to visit him in Shanghai, and he was very pleased. I asked Gigi to find us a hotel to stay in. He booked one not so far from his university so we could see each other during the evenings.

We were in Shanghai for 10 days. During the day, the three of us went out to visit laboratories and institutes that we thought were doing similar things to our laboratory. In the evenings, Gigi came to visit me at the hotel. The hotel we stayed in was actually built from one of those Air Raid bomb shelter tunnels that were built throughout China during the Cultural Revolution. It was underground and the rooms were small and very stuffy with no windows. All the rooms were equipped with just a bed and a table. There were toilets and bathrooms at one end of the corridor, which were shared by all guests. To stay there was like living in a cave, dark and damp. Lights were on 24 hours a day.

Gigi took me out quite a bit. He took me to a Western restaurant one night where we had roast pork and tomato soup. Another night he took me to a concert. We listened to the Shanghai Symphony Orchestra performing some western orchestral music. We went to see the movie 'Jane Eyre' too, which I really enjoyed and wept all the way through. I admired Jane Eyre's strength and perseverance. She had such a terrible childhood, but she survived and became a stronger person. Her romance with Rochester fascinated me, too. I was full of emotion after the movie, but I could not say anything to Gigi. I didn't know how to, and he wasn't sensitive enough to notice and ask - or maybe he didn't know how and what to ask.

Most nights while I was in Shanghai we just stayed in my tiny room and talked. I enjoyed our conversation then. During the entire period, we didn't even hold hands. I was expecting that he would make the first move, but he didn't. He didn't show any signs of affection, so I was disappointed again and left Shanghai with sadness.

Shanghai was 22 hours by ship from Wenzhou where my grandma was living. It was Grandma's 70th birthday, so I decided to take a few days off work to go to Wenzhou to see Grandma. I had such fond and warm memories of Wenzhou. It was there I spent 10 years of my childhood with grandma. It was there I became a gymnast, reached a high standard, and won medals provincially and nationally. Whenever I had a chance, I always wanted to go to Wenzhou.

Relatives and friends in Wenzhou organized a birthday banquet for Grandma. She was very happy to have me there by her side because she was living in Wenzhou on her own.

The last grandson she brought up, my older brother Miao, had moved to Hangzhou, the capital city of Zhejiang province. There was now no one from our family living with her.

I bought Grandma a cardigan with a black background and burgundy floral patterns. She said the colour was too bright for her, but I knew she liked brightly coloured clothes. She only said that because she didn't want her neighbours to say anything about her liking beautiful clothes. I insisted that she wore that cardigan on her birthday, and she did. Everybody said how good she looked in that cardigan. I could see the bright smile on her face, which remains in my memory to this day. She was really happy.

I wrote a letter to Gigi when I was in Wenzhou. I told him that I was a bit disappointed that he didn't seem to show much appreciation on my visit to Shanghai and I felt sad. Then I left Wenzhou for Hangzhou, where I had most gymnastic competitions, to catch a connecting train to return to Guangzhou. I had contacted my favourite Coach Jiao earlier on and she invited me to stay at her place for a few days before I went to Guangzhou.

The bus took 10 hours from Wenzhou to Hangzhou. The winding roads, the mountains and the creeks were still the same. I had been on this road so many times. But the breathtaking scenery and its beauty never ceased to amaze me.

As soon as I stepped out at the bus station, I saw Coach Jiao standing there beside her bicycle. She smiled at me. That lovely smile again! It had been ten years since I last saw her. That was my last competition in Hangzhou when I represented the Wenzhou gymnastics team. I failed her expectation at that time due to having had no coaching that year. She looked a lot older with wrinkles around her eyes, but her face was still very pretty. She was 40 then, and married to that handsome basketball player *'Uncle Chen'* for over 10 years at the time. They had no children.

Coach Jiao lived in an apartment on the outskirts of Hangzhou. She had stopped coaching gymnastics. Instead, she became an aerobics gym coach. That afternoon she invited Chen Xiao Hong, one of the gymnasts who also participated in the national gymnastics competition in 1974 (we were in different age groups, but represented the same Zhejiang province), to her place to meet me. We talked about the training, the competition, the sightseeing in Suzhou, and so on, which left fond memories in us, particularly in me. Chen Xiao Hong had stopped training long ago. She did not go to university or college because her score was not high enough. She was waiting for a job and became one of the *'Waiting-for-job youth'* generation.

In the evening, 'Uncle Chen' came back. He had become a basketball coach. He and Coach Jiao cooked a meal for me, and we had a lovely time together.

On the second day, at 6 o'clock in the morning, Coach Jiao knocked at my door. I was half-asleep. She said there was someone waiting to see me. I couldn't believe my eyes when I saw Gigi standing outside the front door with his bags.

'What are you doing here?' I asked him.

'I have something to do here in Hangzhou,' he replied.

Coach Jiao and 'Uncle Chen' left us alone in the living room. Hangzhou was only two hours away by train from Shanghai. When Gigi received my letter from Wenzhou in which I told him that I was going to stay at Coach Jiao's place for two nights, he made up his mind to come to Hangzhou to see me, to prove that he did appreciate my visit to Shanghai, he said.

'How did you find out Coach Jiao's address?' I asked him. I was still in shock.

'I went to the Sports Institute first. They gave me the address.'

'What if you couldn't find coach Jiao's address?' I wouldn't let it go. *'Hangzhou is such a big city; you are such a fool.'* But I was very happy to see him.

Hangzhou is a beautiful city. There is a Chinese saying describing the beauty of Hangzhou. It says, *'There is heaven above, but there are Suzhou and Hangzhou on earth.'* The famous West Lake is in Hangzhou.

There were many places to see in Hangzhou. We decided to visit Nine Creeks which was situated outside the city.

It was a spring day. Quite cold, with a fine drizzle. We walked hand in hand along the creek for a few hours with not a single person in sight. The rain wet our hair and our shoes became damp by walking in the mud, but our spirits were high. Gigi brought his camera with him and took some photos of me. They were my earliest coloured photos and I looked happy and content in those photos.

Gigi slept on the sofa at Coach Jiao's place that night. On the second day, I had to leave for Guangzhou. Gigi saw me off at the train station. We both stood at the door of the compartment silently. I felt sad and yet happy. Sad because I had to leave Gigi and go back to the city I disliked and where I had no close friends; happy because I knew now that he did care. For the first time in my life, I felt I was wanted, and it was such a warm feeling. It was after this meeting that I told myself, yes, he was the one I wanted. I wanted to marry him. With mixed feelings, I stepped onto the train and waved to Gigi from the window.

Germany

Visiting and working in West Germany - 1986. This is a touristy town that I don't remember the name of.

I continued working and writing to Gigi. Every winter and summer holiday he would come to Guangzhou to visit me. Father wasn't happy with my relationship with Gigi, partly because he didn't know him. He said he noticed that Gigi left things everywhere in the house when he stayed at our place the first time. *'He mustn't be a tidy person,'* he said. He always noticed tiny things like that in life and was critical of them.

But I didn't care. In the evenings when Gigi came to visit me, we would go to the nearby Yue Xiu Park. Because I was living with my parents, there wasn't a private place for us. In fact, in Guangzhou, people's living places were very small and often two or three generations lived under one roof. There were no quiet places for young people like us. Many couples would rather pay to go to the park for some quiet time. In the evenings, there weren't many visitors there to disturb them.

Gigi and I often went to the Yue Xiu Park. It was very close to my parents' place so we could walk there within five minutes.

We would sit up in the hills and talk until the parkkeeper kicked us out with his torch. The parkkeeper must have known every corner and hiding place, we thought, for not once did we escape his search.

In 1986, our laboratory was nearly set up. We purchased some equipment from Germany through Gerhard's laboratory - VDE Institute. There was an agreement drawn between VDE and our laboratory. We would purchase equipment through VDE and VDE would provide training for our engineers.

In August 1986, VDE sent an invitation for 10 engineers to go to Germany to learn how to use the equipment and testing methods in different areas. Our laboratory sent six engineers plus four leaders who knew nothing about testing.

Our German partners were not very happy when they found out that four out of 10 people were not engineers. Not only did the four officials take places that were supposed to be for engineers, but also the German side had to provide entertainment for them. What would they do while we were working during the day? They couldn't speak a word of German or English. We had to give them an interpreter as well. Our official interpreter Mr Zhou, whom we played tennis with while Gerhard visited China, was also a technician working in the testing area. While he was away with the officials, I had to translate for the other four engineers who didn't speak English. In the end, there were only four engineers who ended up doing what they were supposed to do. I didn't spend much time in my area, which was radio interference testing.

We were in Germany for 20 days. We stayed in a small town called Heusenstamm, a quiet, historical, and beautiful town. There were only three policemen in the town, one of the engineers from VDE proudly told us. It was very safe.

You could walk around the town on foot. During the day, we worked at VDE. There was an engineer who lived in the same town who would come and pick the eight of us up in a van. Another engineer gave the other female engineer and me a lift every day. I felt that women were treated well in Western countries, whether it was out of politeness or other reasons I couldn't tell. I didn't live there long enough to know. If it were in China, our group leaders would be sitting in a sedan car rather than a van.

I was surprised to find that VDE had flexible working hours. Each day between 10:00 am to 2:00 pm all staff had to be at work. Other times, people could choose to come earlier or later as they liked, as long as they maintained the required hours each month. I thought this system was fantastic. It provided some flexibility. I didn't like rigid working hours at all.

We finished work at 5:00 pm each day. After work, there wasn't much to do during weekdays. To save on the living allowance that we were given, we often just had instant noodles in the hotel room for dinner. There was a restaurant in the hotel, but we only used it once.

After staying in the hotel for 10 days, we felt that we should make a contribution of some sort to the hotel. We decided to try the restaurant out. The 10 of us sat down one night and we looked at the menu. With my limited English, I helped translate the menu for others. We didn't understand much of it. But I remember I ordered a fish dish. When it came, I couldn't eat it. The smell put me off right away. I barely touched the dish and left the table. My colleagues didn't finish their meals either. We came to the conclusion that Chinese food was far better than German food. Later I learnt that German cuisine was not the best in the world.

So, we had more instant noodles for dinner after that.

The town was so small that there wasn't much to see after a few days of exploration on foot. There were a few buildings that looked historical and beautiful, so I visited them. I didn't know what they were for. All the information was in German, which I didn't understand a word of. There were few people in the streets; I hardly met anyone. There was a small church near the hotel where we stayed where I often went after work, around 5 o'clock. The door was open all the time. Sometimes there was a service, but most times when I paid a visit there was no one at all. When there was a service, I sat in the back row listening to people singing or just observing. I had never been to a church before in my life. It was fascinating to me, to watch people praying and singing songs together. I didn't understand what was said, of course. I felt the quietness and calmness that I never felt before. It seemed that there was nowhere else in the world, in my life, where I had felt so close to something - I could not put it into words. It felt like I had been looking for something all my life and now I had found it.

I just sat there, listening to the sound of the silence. The bell rang at times.

The engineer who lived in that town saw me a couple of times in the church. One day he couldn't help himself; he came up to me after the service and asked me if I was a Catholic. I didn't know what he meant by Catholic because I had no knowledge of any other religions in the world as we were not taught that at school. But I knew it must have had something to do with religion, so I said no. He looked a little bit confused. He must be wondering why I came to the Catholic church not once, but many times, and I wasn't Catholic.

One of the engineers at VDE had a wife who was from Taiwan. He said she often felt lonely, so he wanted to invite us two ladies to his home to meet his wife one day. I asked our leader if it was all right that we accept the invitation. But he didn't like the idea. The reason he gave us was that we didn't know her. Of course, we didn't know her. I thought to myself. That's why we were invited to meet her. And we could speak Chinese to her and make her feel at home. I was not happy with the leader's decision and yet, I couldn't do anything about it. I thought he was rude, arrogant, and most of all, he was jealous because he himself wasn't invited.

Our leaders requested a visit to the Chinese Embassy in Bonn, German's capital city then, which was four hours away from where we stayed. They said they wanted to report some issues to the Chinese Embassy. So, Gerhard and one other engineer, Dr Farklan, drove us to Bonn one Saturday.

On arrival, the group leaders decided that the issues were not important, and they didn't need to visit the Chinese Embassy. Gerhard and Farklan were not impressed by this change of mind. They said they had driven all the way there because we wanted to report to the Chinese Embassy and now, we didn't want to go. *'No, you have to go and see them,'* they said.

So, we went in and sat there for about 5 to 10 minutes, talking about nothing. I didn't understand why we had to go to the Chinese Embassy. There was nothing we needed to tell them.

And then we came out. There were a few hours to spend before we headed back to Heusenstamm. Gerhard asked us what we would like to do since now we were in Bonn. I had always liked Beethoven's music and knew he was born in Bonn, so I said I wanted to visit Beethoven's house or museum. Other members in the group just wanted to sit down and have some German beer. I noticed that Gerhard and Farklan exchanged a few words and the next minute, Gerhard and I were walking alone in the streets. He said he told Farklan to take the rest of the group to a pub and have some beer, pretending that they lost Gerhard and me, so Gerhard could take me to visit Beethoven's house. He knew if I was going to ask the group leader for permission to let me go alone with Gerhard to visit places, he would say no. I was very grateful to Gerhard and also felt what we were doing was very funny. Even Gerhard knew that our leaders didn't like me exploring other things. *'What sort of policy is this?'* I thought to myself. *'What are you doing in Germany if you just want to drink beer? Go back to China. Not only did you take an engineer's place and produced more work for our partner and us, but you stopped other people from seeing places.'*

For the first time, I understood why I always felt frustrated in China. I didn't like the system where people in certain positions could use their power to interfere with other people's lives, and there was nothing you could do to change it because your career, your housing, and your salaries were all in their hands. *'I like West Germany,'* I thought to myself. *'I like western countries, no matter what the Communist Party says about the West.'* The people seemed to live free and happily. They could choose what they liked to do with their lives, while in China, we didn't seem to have much of a choice. A seed was planted in me then; the seed that one day I'd like to live in a Western country.

Our German trip came to an end very quickly. 20 days passed in a flash. I was very sad that we had to leave Germany. Germany was like a dream world to a girl like me who had grown up in closed-off Red China and had never seen the outside world. It was actually a shock to know that Western countries (to me, Germany represented the West) were so beautiful and clean; people were friendly, polite and happy. Nothing like what was written in our books that said people in Western countries were poor; employers (capitalists) tried to squeeze every drop of blood out of their workers.

Gerhard gave me a tape with some of my favourite songs on it as a gift. What made it special and precious was that he sang those songs himself and recorded them. The tape followed me around wherever I went while I was in China. It was like a hope; a hope that one day I was going to live in a country where I could choose what I wanted to do and where I wanted to go without asking any person's permission.

Getting Married

While I was in Germany, Gigi graduated with a master's degree from Shanghai. Before the completion of his study, we discussed where or what he could do for a career. Originally, he was thinking of going to Shenzhen University in Shenzhen, the border city of Hong Kong which was about two hours by train from Guangzhou. Shenzhen University was a newly established university. Gigi wanted to become a lecturer there. Since there weren't many old professors there, he might be able to get promotions faster. But I had a different idea. I wanted us to be together because I couldn't stand this long-distance romance any longer. I was 25 years old and wanted to get married and have a family of my own. Having a warm and loving family had always been my dream ever since I was 15 years old, since I came to Guangzhou. I loved him and wanted to marry him.

I insisted that Gigi come to Guangzhou. At first, he resisted the idea. He was always a career-driven person. He had just graduated from school and had not started a career yet. Shenzhen University seemed to be a good place for him to start, he thought. But I insisted. I went to South-China University of Technology where I did my four-year study and talked to a friend who was a lecturer in the Department of Architecture there, to see if there was a vacancy for Gigi. To my surprise, the department was very interested in Gigi and promised him a position straight away. Gigi finally agreed to come to Guangzhou. Later in our marriage, when we had arguments, he often regretted that he gave up his career for me.

Gigi came to Guangzhou in September 1986. The University

gave him a room sharing with another fellow. The University was on the outskirt of Guangzhou. It would take about an hour and a half by bus to get there. I couldn't visit him during the week because of work, but I would visit him on Sundays - we worked six days a week then.

In December 1986, six months after Gigi moved to Guangzhou, I found myself pregnant. I was afraid. Pregnancy before marriage was considered a terrible thing in China. Not only would I be labelled a bad girl in other people's eyes, but also the government would punish me because sleeping together before marriage was, officially, illegal. I might not have been put in jail, but in other areas of my life such as the increase in wages and housing, the officials would make my life as difficult as they could. Life was already difficult as it was. Why would I want to bring a child into this world to suffer? So, I decided to have an abortion. Gigi agreed wholeheartedly. He wasn't ready for any commitment and responsibility.

The first time I went to the hospital for a checkup one of the nurses asked me if I was married. I was too honest to tell a lie, so I said no. Then she asked me if my workplace and my mother knew about it. Although I knew this had nothing to do with my work and my mother, I told her that no one knew about my pregnancy. I didn't realize that telling her the truth put me in a very unfortunate position.

The second time I went in to make an appointment for the operation, the same nurse said she had to inform my parents and my workplace. I said I prefer them not to know about it. It was my partner's and my business, with nothing to do with anyone else. She made a sign by using her fingers to indicate something. At first, I didn't understand. She did it again and at the same time, she whispered '*money*'. What?! I was puzzled. Public hospitals were free to Chinese citizens who were working at the time. I didn't understand why she had asked me to pay her. And then when I realized what she was asking me to do, I was shocked. She was asking me to give her money under the table; otherwise, she would let my parents know and report me to my workplace.

I could not believe my ears! Here we are, in a communist country where we have been taught that our purpose in life was to serve its people, and here she was, working in a government hospital, threatening me. If I did not give her money, I would get myself into lifelong trouble. I was so humiliated and angry that I was speechless. I left the hospital without making an appointment. Such a corrupted system! How dare she ask for a bribe openly like this, under the bright sun! I could not let this happen. Who gave her permission to do such a thing? How many innocent girls had she threatened? What about the other nurses and doctors in the hospital? Were they all like this?

But time didn't allow me to find out, and I didn't want to put myself to the test. I needed to have the abortion before it was too late, so I went back to the hospital and stuffed 40 dollars into her hands. She put the money into her pocket and led me to the waiting room. I didn't even have to wait for long.

There were a few people in the waiting room. While we were waiting, we could hear the screaming that was coming from the operation theatre. Abortions in China took place without anesthetics. Because of the one-child policy, people who were pregnant with a second child were forced to have an abortion. It took approximately half an hour to do one person: shorter than a haircut. I almost felt numb while I was waiting, I didn't know what to expect.

Finally, after who knows how long, it was my turn. I walked

into the room. I saw two beds in the middle. Around each bed, there were a few women in white uniforms.

'They are doing two people in one room,' I thought to myself. A woman who looked like a doctor asked me to lie on one bed. She told me to relax so they could put the equipment in properly. I felt a cold metal-like thing that was inserted into me. Then the pain started. It was excruciating. It felt like my flesh had been scraped out from my body while I was alive. It was painful enough for people who had already given birth and was even more so for me. One of the nurses tried to talk to me to relax me. She asked me how old I was and what I did for a living. I could hardly spit the words out between my teeth. She said if I tensed up my muscles like that, the doctor would not be able to clean it all out, and if that happened, I would be in more trouble. *'How could you relax your muscles when you were being cut alive! You tell me,'* I said to myself. I tried not to scream. Perhaps I did, perhaps I didn't. After a long, slow period, I heard one of the voices saying, *'Get up! You can go now.'* I pulled myself up, trying to get off the bed, but I couldn't. The pain was so severe that I couldn't move my legs. The doctor who operated on me felt so sorry for me that she helped me off the bed and supported me to a bed in another waiting room. The nurses just stood there watching.

I didn't know how long I lay there. No painkillers were given to me to reduce the pain. Eventually, the pain reduced. As I slowly walked out of the room, I saw the nurse who asked me for money. She said that someone was waiting for me outside and must have gotten worried since it took so long. All my strength was gone. I said nothing to her. I felt sorry for her, having to ask for money in such a way, almost like a beggar. After all, doctors and nurses only earn less than one hundred Chinese Yuan a month. There used to be a saying in China -

people who cut someone's hair earned a better living than a doctor who operated on people's heads.

Gigi and I took the bus home. He was quite supportive and was by my side through the whole thing. I was relieved that the whole ordeal was over. We could get on with our lives.

In 1987, there was an opportunity for me to transfer to an Institute next to Gigi's university. It was the Number 5 Institute of National Electronic Ministry. One of my university schoolmates worked there. I asked her if she could ask whether the Institute would like to accept me. In China, jobs were given by the government. No vacancies were advertised anywhere. The head of my friend's department, which was Safety Testing for electrical products, was a friendly fellow. He knew that I had been to Germany and was exposed to new equipment and technology in the testing area, and he knew my English was quite good. At the time, they had some contacts with USA laboratories and needed someone who had knowledge of testing and English. He said he would like to have me in his department, so I applied for a transfer from my old Institute. It didn't take Mr Liu, who went to Germany as a leader with our engineering group, too long to consider my release. He probably couldn't wait to get rid of me. Apart from my free spirit while we were in Germany, one other reason why Liu didn't like me was because he approached me several times and asked me to apply to become a communist party member. He was in charge of recruiting members. I refused. After what happened during the Cultural Revolution, who would want to join the Party? My father was a Party member; look what happened to him! Look at the corruption in the hospitals! The doctors and nurses had to ask for money from the patients. What good things had the Party done to China and its people after over 35 years of rule? I didn't want to be a member of that kind of Party.

After that, Mr Liu hardly talked to me anymore.

My transfer went smoothly. No 5 Institute was very close to Gigi's University. It was a community of its own, with over a thousand staff. It had a canteen, a medical clinic, a shop, and even a fresh meat and vegetable market. The Institute provided me with a room shared with three other girls. I longed to have a place of my own, staying away from my parents. Although it was a shared place, I still had the freedom to do my own thing without having to worry about my parents' interference. And of course, I was close to Gigi. I could visit him in the evenings, not having to wait until the weekends.

Although Gigi was supposed to be sharing with another colleague, his roommate never turned up, so we almost had a room to ourselves. We didn't have much furniture. All we had was a single bed, a couple of small desks and stools, and a couple of bookshelves. The University provided this furniture. There was no kitchen in the dormitory buildings. Toilets and shower rooms were all shared. Life was quite simple. We didn't have to cook. We ate at the university canteens or my Institute canteen. Therefore, we didn't even have to shop.

Gigi only had to teach for two mornings. Most of the time he read or prepared for the lessons. I was working six days a week. Sometimes I envied him because he seemed to have the freedom that I always wanted.

We decided to put in an application for a flat through my Institute because the chances were better through my workplace than Gigi's University. There was too many staff at the University. We knew we would have to be over 40 when it came our turn to have a flat of our own. A single person simply would not have any chance of getting a room of his own. Only married couples could apply for housing.

So, Gigi and I decided to get married. That was to say, we decided to obtain the marriage certificate through the registration office first. We would not have our wedding ceremony because we didn't have a place to move to yet. Getting married and waiting for a place to move into was a very strong reason for my Institute to consider giving me a flat.

We obtained our marriage certificate on the 5th of February 1987 and then waited for a whole year. Finally, after numerous visits to relevant personnel's homes and almost begging them to consider our case, we got our one-room flat. It was a very old flat with one single room, sized about 18 square meters. It did not have a living room, but it had a separate kitchen, a bathroom, and a tiny balcony.

We were thrilled. Finally, we had a place of our own. The most precious thing was we had a kitchen and a bathroom to ourselves.

Immediately we started to plan and transform the flat into our home. Gigi and I had very similar tastes. It didn't take us long to design the furniture. As an architect, Gigi was good at drawing. I would tell him what I wanted, and he would draw it. We both enjoyed the whole process. Gigi even made a model of our new room with all the furniture we designed in it so we could see what it would look like when it was finished. I liked a bright and clean look to our room, so we decided to have all white furniture. I managed to get a good deal of chipboard through a friend of mine, and we asked a carpenter to make the furniture.

I had already saved some money after five years of working and living with my parents. Gigi didn't have a lot to offer financially because it hadn't been long since he started to work, but this didn't worry me. Money was never an issue to me. Not because I was rich, but because I always cared about things other than money. I longed to have a family of my own, and now my dream had almost come true.

The carpenter finished our furniture in two weeks. By the end of the two weeks, we had a double bed, a wardrobe, a chest of drawers, a desk, a TV unit, a coffee table, and a shelf for Gigi's big drawings.

Gigi painted the furniture by himself, carefully. He was a perfectionist. He painted each piece of furniture three times; each time he would sand it back before the next coat. The furniture was designed to suit the room. Apart from the wardrobe, all other pieces were low units. They fitted the room perfectly, and the room actually looked quite large. We separated the room into two sections. The front half next to the door was our living area. We chose our sofa carefully, too. They were small and simple single pieces combined but could sit five to six people.

The inner part of the room was our bedroom and our study. There wasn't much space left for us to dance, but we could do everything in this room comfortably. If Gigi wanted to read in the corner where our desk was, I could still watch TV at the other end of the room quite privately if I turned the volume down. Gigi's parents gave us a colour TV and a ceiling light with an orange-coloured lampshade. We laid vinyl on top of the concrete floor. In the evenings when we switched on the light, the orange colour light shone into every corner of the room. Our room looked so beautiful and warm, which was exactly what I wanted.

We still didn't have many utensils in our bathroom and kitchen. In fact, the bathroom only had a shower and a toilet. No sink or bench tops. We bought a tiny single-door bar fridge that had no freezer for our kitchen. We didn't have a washing machine. We had no hot water system. We were very fortunate to have a place of our own and we loved it.

Gigi and I in our new home.

Finally, on 30th January 1988, which was also Chinese New Year's Eve, we had our wedding dinner at my parent's place. I insisted on a small wedding. It was never my intention to spend lots of money on a wedding ceremony. Neither Gigi nor I had many friends in Guangzhou. Gigi's father was in Yemen at the time; his mother was in Xi'an looking after his two sisters. My two brothers were away, too. So, there were only my parents, Grandma who was in Guangzhou for her treatment for her thyroid cancer, Gigi's aunt and her husband as representatives from his family, and us - seven people. Grandma was upset with my parents. She said that they didn't give me a proper wedding. She has never seen such a simple wedding like this in her life. But I told her that it was our idea. *'Still,'* she said, *'weddings should be parents' responsibility.'* And it was the first in our family, she said!

Grandma made 10 dishes for our banquet. *'You have to make the most out of it,'* she said. My dearest grandma!

After dinner, Gigi and I took a bus to our new home. It was Chinese New Year's Eve. There weren't many people on the bus. In fact, there weren't many people in the streets. People all went home to have their New Year's Eve with their families. When Grandma heard that we took the bus to go home later she laughed again. This was new to me, she said. *'A bride should be taken in a decorated car, not by bus!'* But I was happy. I was a married woman, and I had a warm home to myself. That was all that mattered.

After our wedding, Grandma and my parents came to our new home for a visit. Behind us is the front gate of South China University of Technology. Our home was not far from the university.

Mother and Father at South China University of Technology, while visiting our new home. They toured around the University as well.

Australia

In 1987, two of my university friends, Hong and Dong, left China to study in Australia. Dong enrolled in an English course in one of the private colleges in Sydney, while Hong and her husband, Yong, enrolled in a similar course in Perth. Hong and Yong actually planned to get married that year. They bought all their furniture for the new home and had their wedding arranged until they heard the news that it was very easy to obtain a visa to study a course in Australia. They decided to cancel their wedding ceremony but still obtain the marriage certificate from the Registry Office and then go to study overseas. Travelling overseas was always difficult in China. Without a direct family member's invitation from an overseas country, an ordinary Chinese citizen could not go to any country for a visit. There was simply no way to obtain a passport. Being accepted by an overseas university or college was the only way for a young person to be able to travel abroad. Even for this, there was an age limit. The student had to have a financial support statement from a relative overseas to prove that all his school and living costs would be fully paid for by this relative. Hong had a relative in Perth at the time. She was able to obtain a statement from her uncle stating that he was willing to pay for Hong and her husband's tuition fees plus living allowance. Dong also had an aunt in the USA who supplied her with the certificate. I was really keen to join them so we could all go to Australia together, but I had no one who could provide me with such a statement. I was enjoying having Gigi so close by after three years of long-distance romance and we were planning to get married and were preparing for our own home. Gigi wasn't very keen on the idea of me paying full fees to study overseas, so I decided to put the idea of studying overseas off for the moment. But my heart went with them.

My married life wasn't as happy as I thought it would be. I enjoyed having a place of my own and loved the home we both created from nothing. But Gigi and I did not get along very well. We both were strong-willed people, and one was more stubborn than the other. We had no idea what marriage, or a relationship, was like. Both of us tried to get the other to listen to our own opinion and hoped that he or I would change. We did not understand why this was happening and, of course, had absolutely no knowledge or necessary skills to cope with the situation. We argued, fought, and battled with cold wars. *'It must be the environment and society that we are living in,'* I thought to myself. Life was still difficult in China. Our wages barely covered our daily food, and we had no money to do anything else. Even if we saved some money from our food, we could not go travelling because there was no such thing as annual leave in China. The longest holiday we had was four days over Chinese New Year. We worked six days a week, and on Sundays, we went to my parents' place. Life was a routine. Every week was the same. I felt bored and my frustration came back again. There had to be a better life than this one, I was sure of that. I was happy when visiting Germany, the year before. I felt freedom. The freedom of being able to express what you feel; the freedom of being able to choose your work, and furthermore, the respect of a human being for another.

'Go overseas,' I thought to myself. *'I want to see the world. I want to see how other people live their lives in other counties.'* I contacted Hong, who had moved from Perth to Melbourne at the time, to find me a college for an English language course. I didn't know how I could get a financial support statement to show the authorities in order to obtain my passport. But, where there is a will, there is a way - my gymnastics training taught me that.

Gigi did not like my idea of going overseas. He warned me that as an overseas student in Australia, life could be more difficult than we had in China. I'd have to find a job to pay for all my study fees and living costs. I had to keep studying to keep my visa. He said, *'How are you going to get residency there? How many years would we have to wait until we could have a stable life?'* I could not answer. I did not know. *'At least we could try,'* I said. At least there was hope for a better life and I was prepared to give it a go. If all else failed and we could not stay in Australia, at least we would have a few years of experiences. Our English would be much better! We could still come back to China. We would have no problem finding a job, even just teaching English. We could still have our lives back. If we stayed in China, a few years would make no difference in our life. We would still work in the same place and be earning the same amount of salary. Our life would be the same for the rest of our lives.

While I asked Hong to find me an English language college in Melbourne, I encouraged Gigi to apply for a PhD course in Australia and to apply for the scholarships that the universities offered. He also participated in the TOEFL English Exam that was set up for overseas students entering the USA to do tertiary studies. Australian authorities also recognised this exam.

The University of Adelaide replied to Gigi's application first. The Department of Architecture of the University accepted Gigi as a full fee-paying PhD student. But he did not get the scholarship. The tuition fee was $18,000 Australian dollars a year! That was totally out of the question! We could not possibly pay even a quarter of that amount of money! Both of us were earning around 150 Chinese Yuan each month, which equalled approximately $40 Australian dollars. My tuition fee for the English course for six months was a lot less. It was around $2500 Australian dollars for a six-month course. I had to pay the course fee and three months' living allowance, which was around $800, in advance to the college. This was the requirement that the Australian government put on us so we wouldn't have to work while we were studying in Australia. Our life was sort of guaranteed. We would get our allowance back when we arrived at school. The Australian government allowed overseas students to work 20 hours a week. Working more than 20 hours a week was illegal. In making this rule, the government also protected the local full-time jobs being taken away by the students, I guessed.

At the time, Gigi's father had worked in the Yemen Arabic Republic for four years as a visiting lecturer sent by the Chinese Government. He saved all the US dollars given by the Chinese government as his living allowance for four years and lent us $2000 US dollars as support for our overseas adventure. This was traditional. Chinese parents always supported their children, especially if it was for study purposes. My parents lent me ten thousand Chinese Yuan, which was about $2000 Australian. I knew in my heart that it was all of their life savings. When was I going to be able to repay them? Would I be able to make a living there? What was the future that lay ahead of me? I had all these questions and doubts in my head, and yet I did not change my mind!

I exchanged my parents' money for US dollars on the black market and asked my father's colleague who had relatives in Hong Kong to send the money to Hong in Australia (you could not wire money overseas from China then). The English Language College that Hong enrolled me in was called Melbourne Learning Centre, which was situated on Lygon Street, Melbourne. Soon after the school received my money, I received an acceptance letter from the school, which would form part of the documents that I needed to apply for my passport through my work unit. I still needed the legal document from an overseas relative that would state that all my expenses for my study abroad would be paid for. Although I paid all my fees, this document was still essential for my passport application. In desperation, Father asked his colleague who had relatives in Hong Kong if he could get us this statement. We were willing to pay if he could help. In the end, we paid 1100 Hong Kong dollars (which was about 200 AUD) for this piece of paper! Did I feel guilty for having to illegally obtain this statement? No, I did not. It was the system that forces people to find a different way.

The personnel officer at my workplace didn't make the procedure easy for me when I submitted my application for a passport. In China, to obtain a passport you had to go through the personnel office in your workplace. If you were a person who did not have a job, then you needed to go through a government office in your street to apply for your passport. People in those offices could make your life easy or difficult depending on whether or not they knew you, liked you, or if they were in a good mood. The government rules were that, at the time of my application for a passport, I could apply for leave without pay for a year while I was studying overseas. The Institute should keep my position and the flat for me for at least a year. But the lady officer at my workplace didn't like me. She had my passport in her hand and would not give it to me unless I resigned from my job, and moved out from the flat that the Institute supplied. I was angry! Obtaining a passport was the first step. I did not know whether the Australian Embassy in Beijing would grant my visa yet. What if my visa was refused? Not only would I have no job, but we would have to live in the street! What right did she have to be able to control people's lives just like that? Only because she happened to be in that position! I pleaded with her to give me the passport and wait for my visa to be issued; then, I would resign and move out of the flat. Some people suggested that I buy presents and take them to her home in the evening. Then you could keep your flat, they said. But I refused. I refuse to bend my head to such a corrupted system! Gigi and I packed our furniture and luggage. We moved to a very old and dark single-bedroom flat that the University had given to Gigi. It was our good luck that he got this flat in time. We didn't even have time to clean the flat and give it a coat of paint. A few days later, I received my passport.

Our plan was, as Gigi and I discussed, that I would go to Australia first. I would work while studying and save money to pay Gigi's tuition fees for him to join me.

With hope and excitement, I sent my passport off to the Australian Embassy in Beijing, together with all the documents needed. The time was May 1989.

Then a major event happened in Chinese history.

Tiananmen Massacre

The Tiananmen Event broke out in Beijing. Students were on a hunger strike in Tiananmen Square. They started their demonstration in March 1989. Their request was an open talk with the government regarding corruption and democratic issues. When the government ignored the students' request, things became heated. The students went on a hunger strike. They sat in Tiananmen Square day and night. Many starved themselves for more than 20 days and fainted. Ambulances and doctors were in and out of the Square. Ordinary people were very worried about the students on hunger strikes. Still, there was no response from the authority. Soon, workers, farmers, local citizens, and even government bureaus joined in the demonstration. Millions of demonstrators marched on the streets in Beijing and later spread to many other cities in China. They came on foot, by bicycle, by truck, by tricycles, and all sorts of transportation. There were students travelling from universities interstate. Tiananmen Square was the centre of the whole of China in those months. It was on TV every night. We watched the television every day closely to find out what was happening, how many students fainted, how many workers and citizens were marching today, what was the government's reaction, etc. We were all extremely excited.

I joined the students from South-China University of Technology and marched the central streets in Guangzhou. It was about time our ordinary citizens did something about the government, the corrupted leaders, and their sons and daughters. It was an incredible time in China. Most of the citizens were on the students' side. Even the central TV crews were on the students' side. We could feel it when they were broadcasting the news. They broadcasted with excitement. We sensed their support for the students, even though the government controlled the media.

Then everything changed suddenly. Everything changed overnight.

On June 4th, 1989, army troops went into Tiananmen Square and opened fire. Their tanks marched over the tents where the students were sleeping in the middle of the night while everyone was asleep. On the second morning when I turned on the TV, the tone of the news had all changed. I saw the two used-to-be cheerful news broadcasters dressed in total black suits and reading the announcement from the government, motionless. In fact, they were almost in tears. They protested silently on the central TV that was seen all over China while they were broadcasting the government announcement. The announcement said that the government had overturned an anti-revolutionary movement in Beijing. A group of anti-revolutionists tried to overturn the current government. The Party would not tolerate such a movement. A few people were dead, and some were injured during the crackdown, the broadcasters said, including our soldiers. There were no scenes of Tiananmen Square. After the announcement, the TV showed the list of the names and photos of those student leaders and some democratic intellectuals who had appeared on Tiananmen Square frequently prior to this morning. These were the anti-revolutionist leaders who were on the run and would be arrested by the authority when they were found, the news declared. Included were student leaders who were known worldwide and most of whom were exiled to Western countries.

I was completely shocked by the news. All our colleagues at work were shocked. At 11:00 pm the night before, the media was still on the students' side. To me, the whole country seemed to be on the students' side. Suddenly, the hope of a more democratic country had been crushed. It was such devastating news to us ordinary people. The whole laboratory at my work was silent. Everyone was depressed. Tears welled up in my eyes after I saw the news. Where were the students? I wondered. Were they still on the Square when the tanks went in?

We never did find out. The government took control of all media. They never revealed the exact death toll. The public was completely cut off from the truth.

In fact, the Hong Kong-Guangzhou railway line was not far from South China University of Technology. The students knew that Hong Kong newspapers would tell the truth, so some students tried to stop the trains coming from Hong Kong and ask for the Hong Kong newspaper. The trains didn't stop, but people did throw newspapers out of the windows to the waiting students standing on both sides of the track.

We saw bloody photos all over the first pages of the newspapers that had been thrown out of the train. Some reported that 20,000 people died, and some reported that at least thousands were dead. Students passed the newspaper around quickly and silently. If the authorities found out who had those newspapers, he or she would be in trouble.

In less than a day. the bloody newspaper was on the walls, noticeboards outside classrooms, and almost everywhere in the University. Students even set up memorial halls for those who were killed in the massacre. They made coffins and paper flower wreaths. According to Chinese tradition, some students even guarded the coffins to keep the deceased company and to protect the spirit of the dead.

But on that evening of June 5th, there was a rumour saying that the army might enter the university, so all the students disappeared. It was so quiet on the campus that night as if there were ghosts hanging around the buildings and trees.

Things slowly went back to normal at the University. Lectures resumed. Students went back to their classrooms. The library was full of researchers again.

It was under these circumstances that I sent my passport in for a visa to enter Australia. But the whole crew of the Australian Embassy in Beijing were withdrawn back to Australia after the shootings on June 4th, 1989. In fact, almost all foreign Embassy staff left China then. They were uncertain about the situation. When tanks and military weapons go into a city, there's got to be something wrong.

I waited for my visa in vain. There was no one in the embassy. Who would issue me a visa? I didn't know when the embassy staff would return to work, and if they returned, how long it was going to be when they would issue mine, as I knew the mail would pile up for those months. I didn't have a job. I was forced to resign from No. 5 Institute, and forced out of the flat we used to live in. Gigi and I were living on one salary with an uncertain future awaiting us. I was in despair. I waited for three months. Nothing happened. The embassy was still closed.

One day, as I was flicking through the newspaper, an advertisement caught my eye. There was a joint-venture handbag factory in the countryside two hours away from Guangzhou. They were looking for a production manager. They offered a good salary for the right person. I applied for the position and got the job. They offered me one thousand yuan a month, which was a lot of money in those days. Gigi only earned 200 yuan as a lecturer at the university. I accepted the offer. I packed my bags and set off for the factory two hours away from Guangzhou in the country.

The factory was in a very small village between Guangzhou and Shengzhen, the border city of Hong Kong. There wasn't even a name for the bus stop. I was dropped off in the middle of the road and in the distance; there were a few buildings in sight where I found the factory without any problems.

The handbag factory was a family business. The younger brother had a business in Hong Kong selling handbags. He accepted orders from all over the world and had them made in this factory in his hometown, which his older brother was running. All the machinists were village girls from other provinces, mostly from poor and remote villages where they couldn't earn a living. The factory provided dormitories and a canteen for them. They worked from 7 o'clock until 10:00 pm, earning quite a good amount of money compared with ordinary workers in Guangzhou. I was one of the four administrative staff that the factory had, including the director who was the elder brother, Lee. Lee lived in Guangzhou before this factory was opened. His wife and two children were still in Guangzhou. He lived with his parents in a nearby four-storey house, a quite luxurious building in the village. A few foremen and I moved into the fourth floor later. I had my own little room. The other girls shared one. Lee discussed some issues relating to how to manufacture products efficiently, and how to minimise the waste of leather and other materials, with me. I offered my opinions as best I could. I had no idea how to manage handbag production! All I had was good common sense - and that worked. The job was easy and there was no pressure. I met the Hong Kong boss once during the month I was there. He paid a visit to the factory and invited us admin staff to a formal dinner. He seemed quite happy with me working there. This was the first time that I had worked in a private enterprise. Before that, I had always worked in government-run institutes.

The atmosphere was different. I found that I was putting in more effort than ever in this job and was enjoying myself in the process. I knew the boss was directly in charge of my salary. I had to impress him if I wanted a salary raise. The living conditions were very harsh. There was no running water. I had to get water from a nearby well if I wanted to wash my face, brush my teeth, or take a shower. This was not new to me, I said to myself. I grew up in such a condition with Grandma in Wenzhou. For showers, we used a bucket and poured water onto our bodies from it.

One early morning at around 5 o'clock, I woke up with excruciating pain in my lower tummy and I felt an urgency to go to the toilet. I went to the toilet, which was a shared one between all the girls. The pain increased. I looked down and found blood. It wasn't my usual time of the month, I thought. I was scared. I went back to bed and waited until 8 o'clock. That was when we had to start work. I told Mr Lee that I had to go back to Guangzhou as I had to see a doctor. At that point in time, the pain in my lower tummy was so severe I could hardly stand up straight. He looked at me and was quite concerned. He said if there was anything urgent there was a local hospital I could go to. The bus would take two hours to get to Guangzhou. I said I didn't know where the local hospital was. He said he would ask a local girl to take me there. The girl came with a bicycle. She asked me to hop onto the seat at the back and she rode me to the hospital. The hospital wasn't too far away from the factory. I was glad that I didn't have to wait to go to Guangzhou to see a doctor. It would have been very uncomfortable with the pain I was in to wait in the middle of the road for the bus and to sit for another two hours to get to the city. I told the doctor my symptoms. He asked me to have a urine test. It turned out that I had a urinary tract infection. My white blood cell reading was three times higher than normal to fight the infection. I was a city girl - used to treated water from the tap. My body was not strong enough to fight the bacteria that was contained in the local water from the well; that was why I got infected. The doctor gave me an injection of penicillin and eventually the pain reduced. I returned to work in the afternoon.

I continued to work in the factory, trying to get used to the harsh living conditions. It was hard to imagine that I was only days away from going to Australia then. Living in such a remote and backward village, surrounded by mostly peasants with whom I hardly had anything to talk about, I felt totally isolated from the world. There was no TV in my room. All I had was a single bed, a bamboo sheet, a blanket, a mosquito net, and a red plastic bucket. I didn't even have a table or a chair.

At the end of August, just a few days before my 28th birthday, I received a phone call from Gigi. He said my visa to Australia had arrived. What? Really? I could hardly believe my ears. I thought it would take them months to sort out the backload of mail in the Australian Embassy in Beijing after the Tiananmen Event. In fact, I was one of the first groups of Chinese students to be granted visas to enter Australia after June 4th, 1989.

After working for Mr Lee for 26 days, I told him that I was leaving for Australia. He didn't say much. He praised my work and asked the accountant to pay me for my less than a month's salary of 800 Chinese Yuan, which was quite a lot compared with ordinary government enterprise workers who at most earned 200 a month in those days, so I was quite happy.

The next step was to book the air ticket. We didn't book with China Airlines because the airfare was almost double the price of most other countries' airfares. We worked out that the cheapest way to get me to Australia was to take a train from Guangzhou to Hong Kong, and then get on the plane from Hong Kong to Melbourne. We had an American friend named Doug who was travelling in Guangzhou at the time. He often came to our home, and we had become good friends. He heard that I was going to Australia and volunteered to go to Hong Kong to book the air ticket for me. As a Chinese, I could not leave China without a valid ticket to go to another country. Hong Kong wouldn't allow me to land either unless I could prove that I was an ongoing passenger. So, we gave Doug some Hong Kong dollars which we exchanged through the black market and paid his return train fare to Hong Kong. We asked him to book the cheapest airfare to Melbourne; it didn't matter which airline it was with.

He returned two days later with a Philippines Airline ticket in his pocket. *'You have to get off the plane in Manila at midnight, wait for two and a half hours, then get onto another plane,'* he said. Fine. If the cheapest way was by boat, I would have asked him to get me a boat ticket. Money was so tight that I left China with just two hundred US dollars in my pocket.

The Departure

The morning I was leaving Guangzhou for Shenzhen, then I was going to walk across the border to Hong Kong. Everyone in my family was quiet. We were all sad and unsure of what the future held for me. Grandma followed me from room to room as I was packing my suitcase, repeatedly saying, *'be careful, be careful, you are going there alone.'* I burst into tears. I could not bear to look at her. At that time, we all knew she had cancer in her bones, and the doctors could not do any more for her. I knew this could be the final time that I would see my dearest grandma, as she might not live until the day I returned. How I wished that she could live even just a few years longer - until I established myself in Australia, and then I'd invite her to come to Australia to have a look. She would have been thrilled. She was such an open-minded and positive person, and she would have loved to see different places and talk to new people. She may even want to learn English! She had lived through war, poverty, and the Cultural Revolution. How I wished I was able to give her a few years of happy life before she left us, but I knew in my heart that this may not be possible. I didn't know how long I would survive as a full fee-paying student in a country to which I had never been, and where a different language was spoken. What if I couldn't find a job to support myself? My living allowance would only last me for three months. What would I do after that? What if the Australian government would not extend my visa? Well, I thought, I've done it before, when my brother Feng and I moved from Wenzhou to Guangzhou. We didn't know anyone then. We could not understand a word of Cantonese. Our parents did not help at all - but we survived. I was only 14 then. Now I was 28, double the age and experience of when our parents took us back in 1976.

It was time to leave home. Everything was ready. I had my passport with the Australian visa on it in my bag, together with the train ticket from Guangzhou to Shenzhen. I had called a friend in Hong Kong earlier to meet me at Shenzhen train station to help me carry my luggage across the border. I was going to live in Australia, but I could not afford to buy any living utensils. So, I brought all the necessary things from home; clothes for all seasons; a quilt; books; dictionaries; pen and paper; scissors - even a kitchen knife and a chopping board. I had one large suitcase, one small suitcase, a large sports bag, and a backpack plus my handbag. I could not possibly carry this much luggage walking across the border by myself. When I asked this friend to help me, she gladly agreed. Gigi would accompany me to Shenzhen and then this friend would take over. I would have someone with me all the time until I checked in with the flight to leave Hong Kong. Everything had been organised.

I said goodbye to my parents and Grandma. I wanted to give Grandma a final big hug. I wanted to hug her tightly and hang around her for just a little longer, as I knew this could be our last moments together. But I didn't. My tears had not stopped all that morning, which was unusual for me as I hardly cried in my life, let alone in front of my parents. I didn't want Grandma to see me crying and I couldn't bear to see her holding a handkerchief, wiping her tears all the time. It is not the Chinese custom to show any affection to each other, even between close family members. I lifted my bags, turned my head, and quickly walked downstairs.

Downstairs, I heard Grandma calling out my name. *'Ah Min... Zi ji dang Xing'* - be careful.

I could still hear her voice when I walked out of the apartment gate and into the street.

That was the last time I heard Grandma's voice. She left us a year later while I was still struggling to find my feet in Australia.

Feng and Gigi accompanied me to the train station. This was the same station where 14 years earlier Grandma, Feng, and I arrived from Wenzhou. Nothing much had changed, except there were a lot more people in the station.

We went to the waiting room to wait for the train to arrive. Guangzhou is the beginning of the trip, so Gigi and I would have allocated seats. We didn't have to fight to get on to the train like we did when we were in between stops, and most certainly we would have had to stand.

And then we heard the announcement: *'The No.94 train from Guangzhou to Shenzhen has been delayed by half an hour.'*

What? A train is delayed from the beginning of the line? This was unheard of! If we were in between stations, it would have been very normal that a train would be delayed, but from the terminus? We have never heard of this before.

Then came another announcement: *'The No.94 train from Guangzhou to Shenzhen has been delayed for one hour.'*

My heart started to sink. The train was supposed to leave Guangzhou at 10:10 am. I was going to meet my friend from Hong Kong at Shenzhen station at 12 o'clock. There was no way I could contact her now to let her know that I was going to be late. Mobile phones were unheard of at that time.

We were sitting there, waiting in agony for the train and listening to the same announcement repeatedly.

Finally, the train arrived, two hours later. By now, I knew I would not see Ling at Shenzhen station. She could not possibly be waiting for two hours without knowing what was going on. She might even think that I was not coming that day; things were so unpredictable in China.

When Feng went home and told my parents about the delay of the train, Father, Mother told me months later, slumped himself in a chair and could not speak for hours. He was so worried that I wasn't going to make it to the China-Hong Kong border.

Gigi and I arrived at Shenzhen station two hours later at two o'clock in the afternoon. There was no sign of my friend Ling. *'Of course,'* I said to Gigi, *'we can't expect her to wait for us forever. She would have no idea what happened. I will have to cross the border by myself.'*

We walked towards the border customs building, not far from the station. I took some of the books and one heavy dictionary out from my backpack and gave them to Gigi, to reduce some weight. Even just a kilo or two would help.

The customs building was very quiet compared to the train station. It was a Sunday afternoon. I thought there would be a lot more people because some Hong Kong citizens or businesspeople who visit Shenzhen for the weekend would be ready to go home.

It was time for me to say goodbye to Gigi. We looked at each other. We didn't hug each other, or even shake hands, not to mention a kiss goodbye. It was simply not the Chinese custom to show personal feelings in public. Gigi just said: *'Take care. As soon as you get to Ling's place, give us a call.'* I nodded my head and said to him, *'You go first.'*

Gigi replied, *'No. You go first.'*

But I insisted that he walk out of the building first and then I'd walk to the customs counter. So, he did.

As soon as Gigi disappeared out of my sight, my heart began to sink. More accurately, I felt like my heart had been taken out of my body and thrown somewhere. When I put my hand on my stomach, it was not there anymore. I couldn't feel it; I couldn't feel anything!

'What are you doing? Minzhi?' I asked myself. *'You've been waiting for three years for Gigi to come to Guangzhou so you could spend the rest of your life with him. But now you are leaving him again. Are you sure you are doing the right thing by going to Australia? How long is it going to be this time before you can see Gigi again?'* Maybe Gigi was right. I shouldn't have applied to study overseas at all. With all these doubts in my mind, I lifted the two suitcases, one in each hand, together with the two bags on my shoulders and a backpack on my back. I dragged myself to the customs counter.

How I made myself and the luggage cross the bridge to the Hong Kong side of the customs was just a blur. I remember myself and my luggage being pushed forward by the sea of people. All of a sudden, these people seemed to appear from nowhere. I couldn't stop to have a rest because there were people on my back pressing. I couldn't step to the side because there were people on both sides, so I kept moving on.

When I got to Hong Kong Customs, there were long queues in

front of every customs officer. I filled in the forms to apply for a transit visa, then I was led to a waiting room with more than 30 people already waiting. I didn't know what was supposed to happen or how long I'd have to wait. By then it was 4:00 pm and I hadn't eaten anything since breakfast.

Then my name was called, and I went to an interview room. The officer asked to see my passport and air ticket to Australia. Then he asked me what I did before I left China. I told him I was an engineer. He didn't ask any further questions and stamped my passport with a transit visa lasting for two days as my plane ticket indicated I was leaving tomorrow.

By the time I got out of customs, it was dark already. I quickly found a public phone to ring Ling to let her know what had happened. She said she waited for nearly two hours for me. When she didn't see me and didn't know how long she was going to wait she left Shenzhen and went back home.

'How can I get to your place from here?' I asked Ling. I was hoping that she would come to the border to meet me, but it was too far and too late for her to come all the way again. She had a husband and two young daughters to look after, and by then it was dinner time.

I followed Ling's instructions, took a train to the central terminal, and then transferred to another train. Finally, I arrived at Ling's apartment. It was after 9:00 pm by then.

'Is my Australia journey going to be like this all the time?' I asked myself. This is only the beginning! So many obstacles to overcome.

But I'd made it. I'd made it to Hong Kong so far. It couldn't get worse than this. The train from the terminus was delayed for two hours! I hope the flight tomorrow would be on time, otherwise, my friend in Melbourne who was going to meet me at the airport would miss me. *'What am I going to do then? Melbourne is so big; my English is limited; am I going to find her place? If only I didn't have so much luggage!'*

How tiny Ling's two-bedroom apartment was. It was beyond my imagination. The bigger bedroom was only the size of a double bed, plus a small space for a fridge. Ling had a single bed that had another layer underneath, so during the day you could sit on the bed and at night, if you pulled the layer out, it became a double bed. Ling, her husband, and their two-year-old daughter slept in it. The other bedroom was the size of a single bed. There was a bunk bed there. Later I found out that Ling's sister-in-law and her son slept on top, and her husband's younger brother slept in the bottom bed. The so-called living room was actually a hallway/entry. If you put a table there, you wouldn't be able to walk through to the bedrooms. Ling has a folding table for eating, and a folding bed for her older daughter to sleep in. The kitchen next to the living room was just a box. Stove, sink and a little bench top all around, and only one person could fit in the middle to prepare meals or to cook. The entire apartment was only 18 square metres! I thought people's living conditions in China were bad, but Hong Kong was worse.

In order to accommodate me for the overnight stay, Ling's husband had to work a night shift so Ling, her younger daughter, and I could sleep in the double bed. I felt guilty to have put them into so much trouble.

On the second day, I visited the aunt of my best friend from primary school, Wei, and her family. They'd moved to Hong Kong 10 years before. Their apartment was a little bigger than

Ling's, and there were only three people living there - Wei's aunt, her husband, and a teenage daughter.

It was my second time visiting Hong Kong. The first time was in 1986 on the way back from Germany. I didn't like Hong Kong much. To me it was too commercial and too busy; there was not much natural scenery to see. This time, I didn't want to go anywhere apart from visiting friends.

In the evening, Ling and Wei's aunt saw me off at Hong Kong airport. My luggage was, obviously, over the 20-kilo limit, but I told them I was a student and had a lot of books in the luggage. They let me pass without paying any penalty.

The flight I took was with Philippine Airlines. It would stop at Manila airport for two hours and then I'd change planes to fly to Melbourne.

It was 2:30 am when we arrived at Manila airport. When I checked in at the counter before entering the waiting room, I saw the two young attendants looking at me and then whispering into each other's ears. They were quite polite towards me. I thought to myself maybe they had mistaken me for one of the student leaders of the Tiananmen Massacre. It was only five months before that the Tiananmen massacre happened. Many of the student leaders would have been hiding or escaping to somewhere at this time. They probably thought I was escaping to Australia via the Philippines.

It was very early in the morning and there weren't many passengers at the airport. To kill the time, I started writing letters to Gigi, describing Hong Kong, Manila Airport, etc. *'Here we go again,'* I said to myself, *'long distance romance. How long is it going to be this time before we unite again?'*

Then at 4:30 am, I boarded the plane to Melbourne.

'What is Australia like? Will it be as nice as Germany? How will I survive there? Will I be able to find a job to support myself?' With all these questions, I boarded the plane...

Arriving in Australia

In 1991, a year after arriving in Melbourne, I visited the famous Sydney Opera House

On 15 November 1989, I arrived at Melbourne Airport, Australia. It was 7 o'clock in the morning. My friend Hong's husband Yong came to the airport to pick me up. Hong and I were good friends at university. She and her husband came to Australia in 1986, three years earlier than when I made up my mind to join them.

I think I must have been in the first group of Chinese students who were given visas after the 1989 Tiananmen event. When the plane I boarded arrived at Manila Airport in the Philippines, at the transit counter, I noticed a few of the staff behind the counter glance at me several times, and I saw them whispering among themselves. At the time, I thought to myself that those people must be thinking that I was one of the student leaders trying to escape China after the Tiananmen event. They were curious. I just gave them a smile.

At Melbourne airport, the Customs Officer who stamped the entry visa on my passport was kind towards me too. He asked me how long I was going to stay in Australia. I'd forgotten my visa was only for 6 months, and I wrote on the entry card 'two years', as that's what I intended to do. The officer didn't question me at all; he just changed two years to six months for me, and I passed through customs without any problems.

On the plane, I was sitting next to a man who said he was a businessman coming back from a business trip to Manila. He heard I was a student who had never been to Australia before and was relying on this friend to pick me up at the airport. He gave me his business card and a 50-cent coin; he said I should ring him if I didn't see my friend at the airport. I kept his card in my bag for a long time. *Are people in Australia all so kind?* I wondered.

Yong was waiting for me at the exit. I saw him immediately when I walked out of the customs gate. At the time he was a Monash university student, so his time was flexible. *'Hong is working,'* he said. She was working in a clothing factory then.

Yong had an old green Toyota Corolla car. It must have been 15 years old, and green is not my favourite colour, but I thought it was good that Hong and Yong even had a car, after being in Australia for just three years. I hoped I'd have my own car one day.

Yong took me to his home, somewhere in Clayton. On the freeway there, I looked out through the car window at the vast space that extended to the end of the sky, thinking, *'the sky is so blue here, and the grass so green!'* But the freeway had a bit of a rundown feeling with the corrugated barricade on the side. I had been to Germany before, and I thought the freeway in Germany was smoother and cleaner.

Hong had arranged for me to stay at a one-bedroom flat in North Fitzroy. It was a flat rented by her friend Shao Min and her husband at the time. But Shao Min had found a job in Dandenong, and Fitzroy was too far from her work. But they had already signed a lease for a year, so Hong suggested that I stay there and pay the rent to her while they moved to somewhere closer to work. There was another Chinese girl in the flat with whom I was going to share. As a student, I could not possibly have the luxury of living in a one-bedroom flat by myself. The rent then was $78 Australian dollars, which was about 400 Chinese Yuan for which I needed to work for four months without eating and drinking in China. When I first came to Australia, as for every other Chinese coming to the western world, everything had to be converted to Chinese money, so everything seemed extremely expensive.

Shao Min picked me up from Hong's place after she finished work that day and took me to Fitzroy. That's where I was going to stay for the next six months.

I needed to find a job straight away. I had 200 US dollars in my pocket when I arrived. My six months of English course fees were paid, but if I wanted to stay longer, I needed to find money for the next lot of school fees so I could have my visa extended. I also wanted to get Gigi out as soon as possible, so we could be together. That meant I needed to pay for his university fees as well. His university fees were from $12,000 to $18,000 a year, depending on which one he attended!

I asked Shao Min and the lady in the flat to give me some advice as to how to find a job. They said usually newspapers had jobs advertised and you needed to ring them. My English was not very good when I first arrived in Australia. Although, compared to most Chinese students, my language was already better than a lot of them, but I wasn't confident enough to talk on the phone. I decided to try the most primitive way - knocking on doors to see if there were any jobs I could do. I had no idea what I'd do. I never thought I'd find a job in the area I studied at university (radio engineering) because of my English and my commitment to the course, so I never tried.

The morning after I arrived in Melbourne, I walked along Brunswick Road in North Fitzroy, knocking at every door that looked like a factory or warehouse. But no one offered me a job.

In 1989, Australia was having the biggest recession in history since the 1930s. It was Paul Keating's *'The recession we have to have'* time. A lot of factories laid off hundreds of workers; many clothing factories closed because of the tax changes in the textile industry. As I was walking along the streets, I saw many signs outside the factory or office, saying *'No jobs'*, or *'No vacancies'*.

After three hours, I got back to the flat, tired, and feeling hopeless. The lady I shared the flat with, Xiao Xie, said that maybe I could come to her factory the next morning to see her boss. She said her factory seemed to be busy all the time, and she was working overtime early every morning and on Saturdays as well. Xiao Xie worked in a knitting factory making woollen jumpers. Her factory was in Brunswick, not far from Fitzroy. She rode a bike to work every day. I said OK and thanked her.

The next day Xiao Xie took me to see her boss. He was a big man. He looked me up and down and asked me what I could do. I said, *'Anything! I can sew, with a machine or needles* (thanks to my mum who made me sew my own shirts when I was in high school so we didn't have to buy clothes, which would be more expensive), *I can clean...'*.

The boss asked an older lady to take me away. The forewoman gave me a nearly finished jumper and asked me to sew the raw seam on the collar to finish the garment neatly. I did so with ease. The boss asked me to come to work the next morning. That was my first job in Australia.

The next day, Xiao Xie left early because she had to work overtime. Luckily, Shao Min's husband lent me a bicycle, so I didn't have to walk for one and a half hours. I followed the way to where I thought the factory was, but I couldn't find the factory! I rode round and round the streets. Finally, more than half an hour late, I found the factory. The same forewoman looked at me unpleasantly and said, *'What time is it? We start work at 8:00 am, not 8:40!'* I told her that I got lost. Then she asked me, *'how long have you been in Australia?'* When I replied *'3 days,'* she did not say a single word after that.

I worked in this factory for two weeks, sewing collars every day. I was getting good at it and worked faster and faster. Some women in the factory, most of them migrants, whispered that I became the boss's favourite because I was a very quick worker. The former boss's favourite girl got jealous, and I felt it, but before she could do anything I had to leave the factory. My English course had started.

The School I enrolled at was called Melbourne Learning Centre. Hong found this school for me. At that time, there were a lot of commercial schools tailoring their courses to suit overseas students, mainly Chinese. Most of the courses were short English courses. Later there were other courses, such as

Computers, Bookkeeping, and so on. None of these courses led to any accredited certificates or diplomas. Such schools were in it for the money, I think.

The school tested our English and put us in different classes according to our results. I and two other girls, who had majored in English at universities in China before they came to Australia, were in the highest class. Later, we were joined by some more students, mostly from China, with some from Taiwan, Singapore, or Korea. Although we only stayed at this school for six months - all of us went to different schools later - a few of us formed good friendships from this class, lasting even to this day. Most of us came without any relatives in Australia. A few had one or two friends in Melbourne. It was very important to make some new friends so our life here was not so isolated. I felt very alone when I first came to Australia. Hong is a good friend, but she had her husband and their lives had already settled into their routine and they had already made a circle of friends from the university. I had nothing, basically. No money, no car, and didn't know my way around. At that time, Clayton seemed very far away from where I lived, so I didn't visit them much.

I still needed to find a job to support myself and to save up for future tuition fees for myself and Gigi.

I contacted a friend of my brother's from Wenzhou. His name is Michael; he adopted an Australian name of course. I knew him from back when we were still in Wenzhou with Grandma. He was in my older brother Miao's class in high school. He often came to our house then, so I got to know him very well. According to Grandma, he and Miao studied together for the entry exams for university in 1977 when China held the first university entry exams after the Cultural Revolution. Michael got into a university in Hangzhou to study English; Miao missed out that year.

It was close to Christmas time, in 1989. My school started on the 27th of November, and Christmas was less than one month away. Michael said I wouldn't be able to find any jobs at this time. Don't even bother trying. Michael was working two jobs at the time. He belonged to those students who came to Australia before the Tiananmen event. The then Prime Minister, Bob Hawke, sympathised with the students' hunger strike in China and gave all Chinese students in Australia, who came before the Tiananmen event, a special four-year temporary residence visa. They didn't need to go to school to keep their student visa valid; they were allowed to work full-time. For Chinese students who came to Australia after June 4th, such as me, we weren't to enjoy this privileged treatment. We had to enrol in a valid course to keep our student visa legitimate, and we were only allowed to work 20 hours a week at most. To work full time was illegal - some students I know of were arrested because of this legal requirement because they worked more than 20 hours a week.

Michael had a day job - working in a curtain factory. After work, he had another part-time job as an office cleaner in one of the St Kilda office blocks. He said he'd ask his boss if there was any vacancy for me. It turned out one of the cleaning staff was going to take the Christmas holiday off for three weeks. Michael recommended me as a replacement for this guy. His boss took a look at me and agreed.

So, I started this cleaning job just before Christmas. I had no idea what I should do. I was in charge of a whole floor that was shared by four or five different companies. Each had its own toilets, kitchenette, and offices. Thank goodness for Michael, who showed me what to do at the beginning, and helped me when he finished his floor upstairs. In the first week, I could not possibly finish the whole floor in three hours. I had to empty all the bins next to every desk, and in the kitchens, clean the sink and worktops, clean bathrooms, wipe the glass doors and vacuum the whole floor - all of these jobs in three hours! After the first week, I got used to it and I actually started to enjoy this solitary work. I even managed to take a rest in their kitchens and steal some biscuits to eat. I could make myself a coffee if I wanted to, but I didn't. *'This is much better than working in the knitting factory,'* I thought. In the knitting factory, there was always someone looking over my shoulder and checking my work. As a cleaner, I only had to work at my own pace, and there was freedom to move around, and no one would really care what I was doing.

There was a construction or architecture company on my floor. I could tell by the drawings on the desks and floor.

One day I came across an employee who worked late. He was still working at his desk when I came in to clean his bin. Looking at those big drawings he spread around on the floor I thought about Gigi. I asked this person, *'Does Australia need architects?'* The reason I asked this question was to find out what sort of future it would hold for us when Gigi came over.

'We need engineers,' he answered simply.

My heart sank, Australia was having a bad recession; it wasn't a good time for Gigi to come, I thought to myself.

The three-week cleaning job finished quickly. I had my first Christmas and New Year in Australia. I don't even remember how we celebrated it. By that time, Xiao Xie, my roommate, had moved out, and another girl had joined me to share the one-bedroom flat. Her name was Mei Yan. Mei Yan was

Michael's friend; she came from the hometown where I grew up, Wenzhou. Mei Yan and I still found the flat too expensive for both of us. We were happy to have another girl move in. In the end, we ended up having another two girls moving in with us, because these two girls didn't get along with their flatmates somewhere else and they didn't want to be separated. They insisted on taking the only bedroom (with two single beds) and Mei Yan and I had to sleep on the living room floor because there was simply no space for another two single beds in this living room/kitchen. As Mei Yan and I had both just arrived in Australia not long before, we had no furniture - no beds, no table, no chairs, and of course, no TV. We only had our sheets and doonas that we brought with us from China. We didn't want to spend any money on luxury things such as beds, because we knew we had to save every dollar for our next round of school fees to keep our visa going. So, we slept on the floor without even a mattress, just a sheet and two Doonas. Later, we picked up an old coffee table that someone threw out and that was our 'dining table'.

We slept on the floor next to the kitchen workbench, and that's where we slept for six months. We had a big plastic sheet to cover our 'beds' during the day, because of the grease from the kitchen - Chinese cooking is very greasy. The wok had to be smoking hot before you poured oil in. By the end of six months, the plastic sheet we used to cover our bedding was all sticky with grease and dust. Luckily, then there was a two-bedroom flat in our block that had been vacated. By then, the four of us were all working and had all saved up some money. We were ready for some improvements, so we applied for the two bedroom flat downstairs, and we got it.

Michael had a stand in one of the Sunday Markets. He helped me with the cleaning job, and it helped me through the Christmas period because I was working and earning money.

When he asked me to help him with his stall at the Sunday Market, I agreed immediately. I wasn't expecting him to pay me; I wouldn't accept it even if he offered, it just wasn't our custom. We always do things for friends.

Michael would pick me up at 5:00 o'clock on Saturday and Sunday mornings and we'd go and set the table up. He was selling watches, clocks, and all kinds of giftware. I enjoyed the experience. Some days were busier than others. You got to meet all sorts of people and talk to people a little. Besides, I was happy that I had some company on the weekends. What would I do if I wasn't helping on the stalls? Hong was the only friend I knew, and she and her husband had their life sorted out long before I arrived. I had no money to go out sightseeing either.

One day on the way back from the market, we drove past a building that looked like a factory or warehouse. On the wall outside it had a sign saying, 'machinists wanted'. We didn't know what sort of 'machinists' they wanted, but we stopped and went in anyway. It turned out that it was a shoe factory. They wanted machinists who could sew shoes. 'I could sew!' I thought to myself. So, I went up to the woman who looked like a forewoman, standing at the front of all the production lines, and asked if they had vacancies. The lady took me to a machine and gave me a piece of synthetic material and a half circle of cardboard; it looked like a lining on the back of the heel of a shoe. She asked me to join them. I looked at the machine. It was very different from the one I used at home. Our home machine was manual and this one was an electrical industrial sewing machine. The threading was different as well. I had no idea how to thread the needles. Luckily, the machine I was sitting at was already threaded. The only thing I had to do was put the material and cardboard together and sew. But I did not know how to lift the damn foot and put the piece under the needle! Manual machines usually have a lever next to the foot and you use that to lift it. But with the machine in front of me, I couldn't find a lever anywhere. Fortunately, the forewoman walked away so I quickly turned around and asked the lady behind me, *'how do you lift the foot up?'* She said, *'use your knee!'* I realized that there was a pedal next to my right knee and when I pushed it sideways, the foot went up! Sewing the pieces together wasn't difficult once I worked out how to use the machine. The forewoman came back and looked at the piece I sewed, she said, *'we are closed for a month during the Christmas period, come back next year. January 22nd. We start work at 6:50 am.'*

That was how I became a shoe machinist. Thanks to my mother again, I was able to use some of the skills I learned under her tutelage.

I worked in the shoe factory (Windsor Smith Shoes, by the way) for the next six months, sewing shoes eight hours a day. I didn't mind the sewing bit, I like sewing, but having to sew on a production line was stressful and tiring. The cut material pieces slowly moved on the belt next to you and you had to finish your part before the next one came. By the end of the day, my neck was stiff, and my back told me I needed to lie down for a while.

During that time there were a lot of Chinese students coming out to Australia and the majority of us had full-time day jobs. The schools were forced to accommodate our situation and opened evening classes because during the day there were simply no students turning up for classes. We all had to work to support ourselves. We would start our lessons at 4:00 pm and finish at 8:30 pm. It was still classified as full-time study, which was what the government required. My day would start at 6:00 am with an alarm clock. I'd quickly have some breakfast - usually a glass of milk and a poached egg, and then I walked for 20 minutes to the shoe factory - Windsor Smith on St Georges Rd in North Fitzroy. We finished at 3:30 pm and I'd take the bus to my English School in Lygon Street. School finished at 8:30 and by the time I got home, it would be 9 o'clock. Then Mei Yan and I started cooking dinner. After dinner, we usually went to bed straight away. And then in the morning I would start another day.

My English course at Lygon street finished in six months. To keep my visa extended, I enrolled in a Business Computer course at Swanston Business College in Swanston Street in the city. This course was for a year.

The great recession was getting worse in 1990, and Windsor Smith started to lay off people. I was one of the latecomers and therefore the first to go. Just before I was sacked, one of the girls in my production line told me that a shoe factory down the road, called Cadets, was looking for machinists. So, I went down to Cadets and found myself a job there - continuing sewing shoes.

I worked at Cadets for another six months, then I left for part-time office work at the college where I enrolled for my computer course. The principal, Mrs Lin, who was a Chinese national and had been in Australia since she was two years old, offered me a 20-hour-a-week job in the college office doing some administrative work. I was hesitant to give up my shoe sewing job because the shoe sewing job was a full-time job, and I could earn more money. Mrs Lin offered me 20 hours of work because she knew that I was an overseas student and was only allowed to work 20 hours a week. She could not possibly break the law and offer me more hours. But the office work was one step closer to what I was looking for, which was one day working a professional job, be it in my own field as a radio engineer or something else in a company office - definitely not in any factories. I wasn't looking down upon the people who worked in factories, where most of the workers came from less educated backgrounds and did what they could. I simply thought I had gone to university and learnt more skills. I wanted and needed to use my brain. Working in factories would bore me to death and was not what I came to Australia for.

For my future's sake, I made a decision to work at the College. It was the beginning of 1991. By then I knew Gigi was not far from joining me on our Australia adventure.

A few days after I arrived in Australia, I went to Melbourne University to enquire about Gigi's application for his doctorate degree in architecture. He applied when I was still in China. In fact, he applied to Adelaide University too and was accepted by the university as a full fee-paying student. But the tuition fee was $18,000 a year! We could not possibly pay even a third of that amount with all our savings, my parents' savings and Gigi's parents' savings added up together. So we had to give that up. Melbourne University's tuition fee was a little cheaper, being $16,000 a year. We didn't know how we were going to get the money, but he applied anyway, hoping that there was a scholarship that he could apply for later.

Gigi's application was rejected by Melbourne University. The reason we were given was that his TOEFL score was not high enough for a doctorate degree. It would be all right for a master's degree, but Gigi had already got a master's degree in China. TOEFL was an international English test that was designed in the United States for international students who would like to study in the US. The score was recognised by Australian universities as well.

When I heard that Gigi's application was rejected by Melbourne University, with a sinking heart, I went to RMIT straight away. I went straight to the Architecture Department. I had no appointment and was wearing jeans and a sporty top, but it must have been my lucky day that day. When I told the receptionist that I'd like to enquire about post-grad study in her department, she said the professor who was in charge of all applications was just in his office that day, and she said she'd ask if he could see me straight away. He did. I gave him a two-page proposal that Gigi had prepared (a housing comparison study of both China and Australia) and told the professor it was for my husband. He read the proposal immediately and said, *'Yes, we'd like to accept him; he can study under me.'*

That was that! He didn't even ask about Gigi's English level, no previous records, no nothing. He said that from Gigi's proposal, he could tell that he had done some study already in China, which he did when he was doing his master's at Tongji University, one of the leading universities in China which was well known for its Architecture department. It turned out this professor was particularly interested in housing comparison studies. Gigi's proposal was just right for his field. I asked the professor for an acceptance letter that we would need to proceed with Gigi's visa applications.

Then there were the fees! RMIT charged $14,000 a year for post-grad studies, which was the cheapest of all other universities in Melbourne. They required us to pay half of the tuition fees upfront.

By early 1991, I had been in Australia for just over a year and I had worked non-stop full-time in the shoe factories for the whole year. I had saved some money. I paid my own computer course fees, and my living expenses were kept minimum. But my savings were not enough for Gigi's half-yearly tuition fees.

Gigi had to ask his parents to lend him some US dollars. Gigi's father had worked as a lecturer in Yemen for four years on a support program from the Chinese government to Yemen. He was given some living allowance while he was there and, as all Chinese people do, he saved his. Gigi borrowed some money and plus my savings, we paid $7,000 to RMIT. Gigi was able to come to Australia to join me, one and a half years after I arrived here.

In the early days in Australia, my weekends were extremely lonely days. I didn't have many friends; I only knew Hong and Michael. The girl I shared a flat with, Mei Yan, found a job in a clothing factory sewing samples for take-home clients.

The boss was Vietnamese and they worked seven days a week, so I only saw her at night when we shared the floor space next to the kitchen.

Although life was not easy in those early years in Australia, I'd worked in factories, as a cleaner, and a waitress, I'd sewed shoes in two shoe factories, and my spirits were high. I had my purpose in life, to work as hard as I could, save enough money, pay up Gigi's university fees so he could come and join me, and then we'd find a way to stay in Australia! I liked Australia. I felt, for the first time in my life, that my life was in my own hands, not anyone else's. There was no one who could do anything to stop me from doing what I chose to do, like those in China: The group leader who didn't want me to see Germany, the woman officer who held my passport in her hand and wouldn't give it to me unless I quit my job and moved out the flat, or the nurse in the hospital who wouldn't arrange my operation if I didn't give her money under the table.

I had finally found the freedom I craved all my life.

Epilogue

I started writing my memoir in 1997, eight years after I arrived in Australia and a year after Gigi and I separated. A good friend of mine, Linda, encouraged me to write down my memories. *'Whatever comes to your mind, just jot it down,'* she said. She also suggested that I attend some personal growth workshops. At the time, there was an organization in Hawthorn called the Augustine Centre, that ran all sorts of personal growth workshops, such as Assertiveness, Exploring Personal Relationships, and so on - not far from where I lived in Kew. The Augustine Centre was a not-for-profit organization run by a few qualified psychologists and counsellors. The aim of the Centre, in my opinion, was to help people with emotional questions (I would say blockages) find some answers and perhaps learn coping skills as they went about living their real lives.

I ended up spending one and a half years with the Augustine Centre, attending different courses and workshops. I was curious; hearing people talking about all sorts of different situations and working out strategies to deal with or solve a dilemma, was new and fascinating to me. Most of the time, by talking about the situation, participants usually came up with a plan or strategy to solve it or understood where the feelings were coming from, by themselves. It was from these workshops I learned that my upbringing and my past had had a great impact on the state of my mind, my thoughts, my feelings, and my behaviors. *'Why can't I be happy? Why do people live? What do people live for?'* These questions had always been on my mind, and I had no answers to them. That was why I could not feel happiness wherever I was and whatever

I had achieved. Since moving back to Guangzhou and living with my parents in a completely new environment, I had no friends, and my parents were strangers at the age of 14. That traumatic change had frozen me from growing up. I could forever feel that 14-year-old self, living inside me, feeling the hurt, the fear, and the need for comfort. I pushed myself to do all the necessary things that were needed to live life, such as finishing school, getting into university and graduating, then working, finding a partner, and getting married. But inside, I was never happy, never fulfilled or content, even though I achieved what I wanted to achieve at the time.

Ever since I was 15, I wanted to have a family of my own. I wanted to make a warm and comfortable home, a place where I could rest my body and mind. I had that. Gigi and I loved each other, and we built our home together. And yet, two years later, I chose to give all this up, leaving my husband and my familiar surroundings again, for a place I knew nothing about and not even its language. Why?! What was I searching for? Would I find whatever I was searching for, and would I be happy then?

In the early months of arriving in Australia, my focus was looking for a job - any job. I only had 200 US dollars on me when I arrived, and the language school returned 800 Australian dollars back to me for the living expenses I paid in advance while I was still in China. My visa was only for six months. To continue staying in Australia legally, I had to keep studying, which meant I needed to keep paying school fees. I also needed to save up and pay for Gigi's tuition fees. I had a purpose; I was very driven then.

Gigi came to join me in Australia in 1992. Australia was experiencing the worst recession in decades. The hardest hit area was the building industry. He could not find a job in architecture and was very disappointed and stressed. At that time, China was booming in their economy; buildings were going up everywhere, *'like bamboo shoots'*, as the Chinese saying goes.

'My students are doing so well and making millions,' he would say. I knew somewhat he blamed me for coming to Australia. We both knew if we had stayed in China, our life would be improving quickly, and we would be making lots of money. But I had no intention of going back. I liked the freedom of living in Australia. No one looking over my shoulder at what I did, or how I lived my life. I had a car; I could go and visit anywhere I wanted. I could do whatever I pleased, even when we were on student visas and did not know what our future held. But where there's a will, there's a way.

We struggled for a few years, with me working here and there. Finally, I landed a part-time job as a Multicultural Aide shared by two primary schools, and later on extended to a full-time job shared by four primary schools. Gigi finally found a job as an architect in an architecture firm.

In 1993, the Australian government had a new policy. All students who came out after the 1989 Tiananmen massacre could apply to stay in Australia permanently. So, Gigi and I applied for Australian permanent residency, and we could finally see our future in Australia. We even bought a two-bedroom old house in Glen Iris in 1995. House prices were not that high then. With the help of a bank loan and no children, we could still do it.

But Gigi and I struggled with our relationship. Neither of us had examples of what a good relationship was like. I had this idea that a soulmate would share the same views in every aspect of life. We did not know that we needed to nurture a relationship and make an effort to do nice things for each other and together, even after we were married. We were so busy focusing on finding jobs and earning enough money to pay the loan off, that we neglected to look after our relationship and each other. Neither of us was happy, but we did not know what to do.

We talked about separation a number of times because we did not know how to save the marriage. It seemed that when we were struggling when we first came to Australia, we had a purpose - to find a good job, earn enough money, and settle down. Finally, when we bought the house, life's struggles eased a little and we looked at each other; we had become strangers. Looking back now, had we both attended the Augustine Centre earlier, before our separation, not after, we may well have been able to save the marriage. After all, we shared similar interests, we came from the same culture, and we shared a lot of similar views, but we could not see it then, or at least I could not see it then.

I initiated the separation. I left Gigi, moved out of the house with a couple of suitcases, and moved into shared accommodation with a stranger. Ironic, isn't it? How many times would I have to leave my family and live in an unfamiliar situation?

Did I intentionally re-create the situation of when my parents abandoned me when I was five? I often ask myself this question. As I mentioned earlier in my Memoir, the trauma you experienced in childhood, if it didn't affect your life then, it would affect your life later. I believe leaving my family and starting new repeatedly has something to do with my childhood experiences. The timing I chose to leave Gigi was, now thinking back, bizarre. At the time I chose to move out of the house, Gigi's parents had come to Australia for a visit from China. They were here for a month. I could have waited until they left and then initiated the separation. But my reasoning was, and at the time I firmly believed, that at least he would have his parents to comfort him! Was that what I wished for myself? I don't know.

Gigi found a partner within a year of our separation. Four years later, I met my current partner, with whom I have two beautiful daughters, Lia and Sian, who have grown to be two kind, intelligent, strong-willed, and at times, opinionated individuals.

Did I regret leaving Gigi and ending my first marriage? I can only say, without the divorce, I would not have taken a hard look at myself or have become more aware of the choices I made later in my life. I would probably still blame my parents for the hurt that Feng and I endured when we went back to live with them.

I have long forgiven my parents for their coldness when we were reunited with them. My parents suffered physically, emotionally, and spiritually. The whole generation of that era endured unbelievable suffering, and this trauma, extended to their children.

At the time of completing this memoir (2022), both of my parents have retired from work. Father is 91 and Mother is 87. They have a few health issues, but their minds are still sharp. Feng and Miao are both living in Guangzhou with their families. They have a son each. Miao continued pursuing his career as a dancer and later became a well-regarded choreographer and show director in China. He was chosen to choreograph the part where China was receiving the Asian Games flag during the Doha Asian Games Closing Ceremony in 2006. He and his dance show, 'Opera Warrior', were chosen to perform in the Sydney Opera House at a closing ceremony for Sydney and Guangzhou Sister City Cultural Week in 2011. We all went to Sydney to see his show and meet him.

Feng was sent to work on a ship as a radio operator after he graduated from the Sailor's College. He worked on the ship for nine years before coming ashore and working in a private real estate company as a leasing manager.

Grandma passed away from bone cancer five months after I arrived in Australia. I could not go back to say goodbye to her as I had just arrived and was struggling financially. How I wished she would have lived longer - at least until I settled in Australia and then, I would have liked to invite her over and stay with me for a while. She would have been over the moon to travel around Australia and see how people live in this abundant and free country. She was always a positive person, always curious about new things. She would have loved Australia.

I have made Australia home. I have no regrets about leaving China, leaving the oppressed life behind. China has changed dramatically since my departure in 1989. People's lives in cities have improved a lot, there is an abundance of food, and no more poverty, at least in cities. People are not so interested in politics anymore, instead, they are eager for money now.

I go back and visit my parents and my brothers as frequently as I can. I have brought my partner and the two girls to meet my parents and brothers. Every time we went back to China, we would choose a city or two we hadn't visited before to visit. We all enjoyed our travelling in China.

I'm lucky to be able to live in Australia. This country has given me a new meaning of life; the life I was searching for all my life - to live my life freely, to be free from anyone's constraint. I have chosen Australia to be my home.

Acknowledgements

There are a few people I would like to thank. First of all, Linda Midalia, without whom this book would not have existed. It was her encouragement and understanding that enabled me to put pen to paper in the first place. Every chapter I sent to her, she would read it with excitement and interest, and then gave me feedback afterwards - even though there were many mistakes as my English was bad then. Talking to Linda about my experiences has been a healing journey for me over the years. All those pains that had been buried inside me for so long have lessened now that they are in the open. So, thank you, Linda, from the bottom of my heart. May our friendship last forever.

I would also like to thank Kaye Nutman, whom I met through a neighbourhood online platform. Kaye volunteered to read my book and correct any errors she found. Kaye has helped several people self-publish their books in the past. She has given me a lot of valuable advice in regard to self-publishing. Thank you, Kaye; without you, this book would still be buried deep in my computer hard drive for sure. Thank you for so generously giving up your time to help me.

My thanks also extend to Irene McKeddie who also gave up her time to read the draft and give me feedback. Irene corrected my mistakes in grammar and tenses as she is an English teacher! Thank you, Irene!

I also want to thank everyone who ever said anything positive to me or taught me something. I heard it all, and it meant something to me. Thank you!

Last but not least , thank you, readers, for taking the time to read my book. If my story touched you in some way or inspired you to tell your own story, I'd like to hear from you. You can reach me via email: janemzxing@gmail.com.

www.ingramcontent.com/pod-product-compliance
Lightning Source LLC
Chambersburg PA
CBHW040240010526
44107CB00065B/2821